Lessons from Generation X to Generation Next

MCKENZIE MCPHERSON

MCKENZIE MCPHERSON

Copyright © 2012 MCKENZIE MCPHERSON

All rights reserved.

ISBN: 0988303124
ISBN-13: 978-0-9883031-2-6

MCKENZIE MCPHERSON

LESSONS FROM GENERATION X TO GENERATION NEXT

This book is dedicated to my parents, Norbert and Joan McPherson, especially my mother, for following through on the vision she had for her children.

It's also dedicated to you, the reader, in hopes that it will prompt you to love people, inspire others, value life, and entertain those you meet—in other words, to L.IV.E a meaningful life.

MCKENZIE MCPHERSON

CONTENTS

Foreword   1

Preface   3

Acknowledgments   7

Introduction   11

Chapter 1: Family   15
- In General   17
- Young People | Teenagers   29
- Young Ladies   51
- Young Men   65

Chapter 2: Parenting   83
- In General   85
- Mothers   115
- Fathers   123

Chapter 3: Education   137

Chapter 4: Career   151
- In General   153
- Employees   173
- Employers   183

Chapter 5: Health   197

Chapter 6: Finances   213

MCKENZIE MCPHERSON

Chapter 7: Relationships   237
- In General   239
- Women   263
- Men   327

Chapter 8: Pop Culture   355

Chapter 9: Life   395

Chapter 10: Spirituality   455

MCKENZIE MCPHERSON

Foreword

Anyone reading this book should savor the moment because you have been blessed with an opportunity to be introduced to genius on the ground floor.

Lessons from Generation X to Generation Next, McKenzie McPherson's maiden work, focuses on her life experiences and observations. As you read, you will be impressed with her maturity and understanding of real-life situations. The genius, however, lies in her ability to not only identify problems but also to dispense advice in a concise manner that makes it easy to comprehend.

As you read, you will have a number of moments when you say to yourself, "hummmmmmm" or even "you know, I've never thought of that." Her advice and observations reflect insights expected of a person with a maturity level beyond her years.

Ms. McPherson has written a wonderfully comprehensive book that has made it easy to identify and understand provocative and vexing social problems that, according to her, often have simple solutions.

Lessons from Generation X to Generation Next is compelling, informative, instructional, and quite easy to read. For a first book, it's skillfully written, asking and then offering solutions to many problems faced by not only young people but also adults in late stages of life. This book will be helpful to anyone wanting to understand and examine the complexities of our time.

Simply stated this is one of the best books I've read dealing with real-life problems and solutions. It has something for everyone and I strongly recommend it.

—Rachford D. Potter
Former high school principal and teacher

Preface

Some people have asked me what makes me qualified to offer advice on how people should live their lives. My answer is usually that I have lived long enough to experience life. I believe that life is an experience that is all about application. The more you apply and equip yourself with good advice, the more constructive your life will be.

When I was younger, my parents sat me down many times and tried to explain the pitfalls that lay ahead if I didn't adhere to their rules. They would consistently reiterate that they were telling me these things not to be the ultimate killjoy but to spare me some very difficult life lessons.

My dad would often remind me and my siblings that, "A hard head makes for a soft behind." In hindsight, it was deep-rooted arrogance that led me to block out most of their warnings. I was arrogant enough to believe that I would live long enough to repair whatever mistakes I made.

Unfortunately, far too many young people—including myself—have displayed a certain level of arrogance, which makes someone of wisdom reluctant to offer advice. I'm sure there have been many times in my life where I have alienated wise individuals, which has been to my detriment.

What I failed miserably to realize was that wisdom comes in many different ages, shapes, sizes, colors, creeds, languages, professions, and personalities.

One of my biggest character flaws is that I subscribe to my

own understanding far too much. If I don't think a person is qualified or fits the image of someone I think should be offering me advice, I completely disregard it instead of being open to learning something new.

People have disregarded me because of my age, and I have disregarded others because of their age, but I've found that wisdom doesn't depend on the chronological age of a person. You can learn something new from anyone and at any time on your journey to your destination.

This book documents my journey and shares the good, the bad, and the ugly with some insertions from people who have influenced me along the way.

This book is not a soapbox for me to preach to the masses. In no way am I trying to tell you how to live your life or how to be a good Christian. I'm presenting my life uncensored and unadulterated in hopes that you will learn something productive.

Even though I'm only in my early thirties, I have spent all my life learning from some of the poor decisions I have made. Why not live vicariously through me?

As imperfect people, we're bound to falter. If we didn't, how would we grow into the people we were created to be? However, we could have avoided some of the bad experiences if had we acknowledged the advice that was being offered.

Wisdom is only lost on the young if we waste our youthful

days.

Ecclesiastes 1:9 says, *"What has been will be again, what has been done will be done again; there's nothing new under the sun."* To me this means that the good decisions we make today were made by our ancestors yesterday and will be made by our children tomorrow, and the poor decisions we make today were also made by our ancestors and will be made by our children tomorrow. These circumstances aren't new to the human experience; the only new variable is the person.

Whether you choose to accept or acknowledge it, our days are numbered and the only legacy we will leave behind is the ability for future generations to learn how to make informed decisions.

When it comes to life lessons, the past is the present and the future. I beseech you to pay attention, learn, and pass along those lessons.

I have written this book in anecdotal format because I believe in getting to the point as soon as possible. I hate fluff and I don't want to think for you; rather, I trust you enough to think for yourself.

In reading this book, all I ask is that you read it with an open mind and heart receptive to learning something new and beneficial.

—McKenzie McPherson

Note: *The thirty-six alphanumeric words are intentional and* *are woven into text so you can solve the puzzle at the end of the book.*

Acknowledgments

People don't know what they mean to you unless you acknowledge them publically. At this stage in my life, this statement is quite relevant; thus, I would like to acknowledge a few people who have been dear and great to me.

The person who has influenced my life the most has been my mother, Joan McPherson. She has never given up on me and has always told me that nothing is impossible; she was right. She has shown me what it means to have vision, for she not only talked about what she wanted to accomplish, but she also planned, strategized, and most importantly executed. If she said she was going to do something, she did it and transparently, too, so we as children could see what it meant to have vision.

My dad, Norbert, has also played an integral role in my life. Through parables, he encouraged me and my siblings to think for ourselves from a very young age. At that time, we couldn't have imagined the roles those parables would play in our adult lives. As my life has evolved, I've at times found myself remembering the stories and beating myself up for not being more inquisitive and asking more questions when I could.

I credit my sister, Racquel, with showing me the meaning of love. According to 1 Corinthians 13:4–7, *"Love is patient, love is kind. It does not envy, it does not boast, it is not proud. It is not rude, it is not self-seeking, it is not easily angered, it keeps no record of wrongs. Love does not delight in evil but rejoices with the truth. It always protects, always trusts, always hopes, always perseveres."* Racquel has always found beauty in my ugliness, and because of that, I know what it feels like to be loved.

My brother, Norbert, has always been there when I needed a big brother to lean on.

Some people are teachers by profession, and at 3:00 p.m. their job is over. However, there are other people who are also teachers, but their job doesn't end at 3:00 p.m. Rachford D. Potter was one of these teachers. His job continued well after 3:00 p.m. not because he didn't have a life but because he genuinely cared about the well-being of his students.

Mr. Potter is now retired but was one of the few educators who understood the impact he could have on the children he taught. The way he taught was very relatable and conducive to learning. Mr. Potter is one of the few educators who has taught me and my siblings; he has known us for almost twenty years and has, I hope, seen the way our characters have changed for the better.

I don't think Mr. Potter will ever fully comprehend the love and gratitude that's in our hearts for him.

John Chancellor, whom I have never met except via e-mail, has done a wonderful job in helping me to stay focused on the positive and exclude the negative.

Raul Sinclair did an amazing job tailoring the coat of arms just the way I wanted it, all while being on a very strict budget.

Many thanks to all my extended family and friends, both foreign and domestic, whose privacy I am respecting. The road we have traveled to get this book published hasn't always been excitement free, but through it all, we have excelled.

Psalm 139:13–16 says, *"For you created my inmost being; you knit me together in my mother's womb. I praise you because I am fearfully and wonderfully made; your works are wonderful, I know that full well. My frame was not hidden from you when I was made in the secret place. When I was woven together in the depths of the earth, your eyes saw my unformed body. All the days ordained for me were written in your book before one of them came to be."*

With that said, thanks to God, for pruning, prodding, and preparing me to share myself with the world selflessly. This book would not have been written without you as my backbone.

Introduction

Advances in technology and the popularity of social networking services like Facebook, Twitter, and Instagram are making our personal lives evolve faster than we can imagine or keep track of.

As a result, some of us don't have time to sit down and reflect on the decisions that we have made throughout the years. Good or bad, these decisions have not only influenced us but those we love.

If you take a few minutes to reflect, you could probably come up with a few anecdotes that describe some of these decisions. Some may be subtle while others may be obvious; nonetheless, they have dramatically influenced the way you live and relate to others.

In the words of H. L. Mencken, *"The older I grow, the more I distrust the familiar doctrine that age brings wisdom."* Even though McKenzie McPherson is only in her early thirties, it's apparent that she has not only attended the school of hard knocks but also learned from some of its valedictorians.

She has compiled those lessons into this wonderful collection of over three thousand anecdotes and truths grouped together into ten different categories: family, parents, education, career, health, finances, relationships, pop culture, life, and spirituality.

Her book offers some real-life guidance to people of all ages that will greatly improve the quality of life for anyone who reads it and perhaps generations to come.

You will get the greatest value not from just reading these anecdotes but also from reflecting on them so that they become a part of the way you think and live. You can achieve this by journaling about them or using them as a discussion guide with your children, students, or a peer group.

As Eleanor Roosevelt said, *"Learn from the mistakes of others. You can't live long enough to make them all yourself."* It's not only wise to learn from our mistakes but generationally advantageous to share what we have learned with those who might be heading down the path we are all too familiar with. Eleanor Roosevelt suggested that we won't live long enough to make them all ourselves and realistically why would we want to?

There are few guarantees in life, but one of the most sobering is that one day we will die, and even though death might capture our bodies, our spirits will forever be liberated in the lessons that we pass on from one generation to the next.

Ms. McPherson has shared a lot of wisdom in her anecdotes—all of which combined makes for an inspiring and thought-provoking read.

—John Chancellor
Mentor and Life Coach
www.teachthesoul.com

CHAPTER 1

FAMILY

LESSONS FROM GENERATION X TO GENERATION NEXT

***

Introduction

Most of us were raised in a family—good or bad, positive or negative. From the start we were indoctrinated that we should love, support, and be loyal to these people, no matter what.

There's no such thing as the perfect family—mine included. I was raised in Jamaica, West Indies, and for the most part my childhood years were similar to most.

Yes, we had familial issues but what family doesn't? I was fortunate to have loving, nurturing, and caring aunts, uncles, cousins, grandparents, and one heck of a maternal grandmother. Since then, I have realized that what I had was a luxury that unfortunately some children never experience.

Through it all, what I've come to realize is that your biological family isn't the only group of people who are capable of loving you unconditionally.

Sometimes, your biological family is far more cruel and unloving than strangers you meet throughout your journey.

To be considered your family, people don't necessarily have to share your DNA, but they must love and respect you just the way you are.

Yes, we all want to be accepted by our biological family, but that isn't always the case. Love comes from different places at different times from different people and should not be disregarded because the bearer doesn't share our DNA.

***
In General

- Your family is what it is.

- The family you have is exactly the family you need.

- **Be grateful for your family because some people don't have any.**

- Millions of families around the world are screwed up just like yours.

- Scars and bitterne19s from family situations can be resolved.

- **READ: "HEALED WITHOUT SCARS" BY DAVID EVANS**

- It's unbeneficial to let scars and bitterness from family situations hold you back from living a prosperous and fulfilling life.

- Rich families also have familial issues.

- **Your biological family isn't the only group of**

people who will love you unconditionally.

- Make time to enjoy your family.

- Every family has a crazy relative, so don't think yours is exceptional.

- To be ashamed of your family is to be ashamed of who you are.

- **If you have unresolved issues within your family, by all means, get professional help regardless of what your family might think.**

- Pain can be emotional and physical; therefore, when you feel it, it's a sign something is wrong. It's senseless to ignore the warning.

- **Family therapy sessions can be therapeutic.**

- Mental problems are not exclusive to a particular group of people.

- Your family might not always be there in trying times, so learn to develop other healthy relationships.

- Merge your biological and church family as best as possible.

- **You might not approve of a family member's partner, but you should still respect his or her choice.**

- The more you disrespect a family member's partner, the more the family member will gravitate toward that person.

- Whether you admit it or not, your family has helped to shape you in a positive way.

- Nothing is wrong with having family disagreements, but airing them in public is despicable.

- **The family environment should be a safe place that is free of fear, molestation, and depravity.**

- ❖ Educate children in your family about molestation and incest.

- ❖ Concealing molestation and incest within the family damages the abused.

- ❖ **If a family member is abusing a child, by all means, seek professional help.**

- ❖ If a prominent person in the commu14ity is molesting a family member, do not accept a payoff to remain silent.

- ❖ Refrain from discussing private family matters with strangers.

- ❖ **People will use you to destroy your family's reputation.**

- ❖ You have a distinctive role in your family; know and embrace it.

- ❖ There is no such person as the black sheep of the family.

- ❖ **Positive reinforcement goes a long way.**

- Unfortunately, family members sometimes act the way they are treated.

- Live your life, but do not be selfish with your time.

- Your family can only drive you crazy if you let them.

- **You can't fix family members; therefore, don't try.**

- Toxic family secrets can lead to madness.

- Your family can be your greatest asset or your greatest liability.

- **Don't allow family members to use guilt to make you think you owe them something.**

- Having an annual family outing is g1515d for staying connected.

- Some family members can be manipulative; it's not prudent to allow yourself to be caught in their webs.

- ❖ **You are lovable, regardless of what your family or others say.**

- ❖ There should be transparency within the family; everyone should know what is going on.

- ❖ Not all family members are trustworthy or loyal.

- ❖ Be wary of family businesses and joint ventures.

- ❖ **Before signing up for a family business, know your cut and make sure it's in writing.**

- ❖ A family business is just like any other business; its primary goal is to maximize profits and minimize expenditures.

- ❖ Your spouse can complicate your role in the family business.

- ❖ Avoid going into business with reckless family members.

- ❖ **If your family and spouse love you, they will try to get along out of respect for you.**

- ❖ If you work for a family-owned business, you should take your job very seriously.

- ❖ You should go out of your way to make each family member feel welcomed.

- ❖ **It takes a family to raise a child.**

- ❖ When your family is doing well, you are doing well.

- ❖ **Encourage and support the dreams and aspirations of family members.**

- ❖ Respect a family member's position in the community.

- ❖ If you receive special treatment due to a prominent family member's connections, don't abuse those privileges.

- ❖ **You are not entitled to a wealthy family member's money.**

- ❖ Treat your family properly and hopefully it will be reciprocated.

- Try to be a positive role model for children in your family.

- **Be loving, respectful, patient, and polite with older family members.**

- Being married is incredible, but still make time for your family.

- You show your spouse how to treat your family by the way you treat them.

- **It's unwise to marry someone who disrespects or hates your family.**

- Listen to your family's doubts when it comes to choosing a life partner.

- **Your family is a microcommunity, so there should be no such thing as *my* children.**

- If it's good enough for your children, then it should be good enough for *all* the children in your family.

- ❖ If it's unhealthy for your children, then it should be unhealthy for *all* the children in your family.

- ❖ **Invest in educational items for children in your family instead of expensive clothing and gadgets.**

- ❖ If you are fluent in a foreign language, by all means teach it to interested family members.

- ❖ **Just because you are living in a foreign country doesn't mean you should abandon the cultural norms of your home country.**

- ❖ Be honest with family members, but in a loving way.

- ❖ **Enabling an addicted family member makes you partly responsible for his or her condition.**

- Tough love is sometimes necessary in complicated family situations.

- **If a family member is wayward, sometimes a little time in jail is exactly what he or she needs.**

- When young ladies in your family are starting to develop physically, be discreet in speaking about their development in front of male family members.

- **When young ladies in your family hit puberty, avoid groping developing body parts.**

- When young men in your family hit puberty, avoid asking them about their wet dreams in public.

- There are pros and cons when it comes to all families.

- **You do not have to share the same DNA to be considered part of a family.**

* * *

Introduction

As I write this, I remember the exuberance of my teenage years when I had so many dreams and possible destinations. I couldn't wait to be an adult so I would no longer be under the ruling thumb of my parents.

One of my biggest pet peeves during this time was that I didn't believe my mother trusted me enough to make my own decisions and the right ones at that. Can you relate?

It got to a point where instead of listening to her, I was simply hearing her. What wisdom she was trying to impart to me went in one ear and out the other.

Like most teenagers, I thought my parents just didn't understand me. I can only imagine what some teens are going through in this digital age with iPhones, Twitter, and the like.

Take some advice from a person who knows firsthand the pitfalls of not listening to one's parents. Most parents know what they are doing and talking about. You must realize that parents have experienced some of what you are going through or will go through.

A good parent usually wants to spare his or her children pain and heartache. Trust me, your parents can deal with their own failures but it's very difficult for them to accept you failing especially when you didn't have to.

While some parents are hypocritical when it comes to parenting, don't have the right answers, and can be very manipulative and controlling, through it all they are your number one fans. No matter what you do, they will more than likely always be in your corner.

If your mother gave birth to you at sixteen, there's a reason she's warning you about unprotected sex. If your dad stole cars with his friends, there's a reason he's warning you about the company you keep.

Once again, parents don't always go about instructing you diplomatically, but I implore you to listen to what they say and ignore how they say it.

Because I didn't listen, I wasted many years and thousands of dollars fixing situations that shouldn't have been broken in the first place.

I'm not telling you these things on behalf of your parents but because I believe that your teenage years set the tone for what your adult life will eventually become.

Some of the decisions that you make now, whether good or bad, will impact you for decades to come, and I want you to invest wisely in your future by heeding the words of seasoned adults instead of wasting valuable time and money.

Young People | Teenagers

- Your parents brought you into the world, but you belong to God.

- **You are fearfully and wonderfully made; it's unwise to forget that.**

- You are a work of art, and there will never be another piece like you in the history of the world.

- Your parents truly love you; however, they might have a hard time showing it.

- **Not all parents know how to demonstrate love; you might have one of those parents!**

- Some parents have a hard time saying, "I love you," but they say it in other ways, like making sure all your needs are met.

- School is for learning not fraternizing.

- ❖ Know your family's financial situation; that is to say, if your parents are struggling to send you to a prominent school, you can't afford to flunk out.

- ❖ **Sex is a luxury only adults with good-paying jobs can afford.**

- ❖ It's unbeneficial to take your youth for granted.

- ❖ If you are a talented student, let your talents speak for themselves.

- ❖ Not every classmate will be happy that you are a talented student.

- ❖ **Embrace your talents without letting anyone make you feel guilty for having them.**

- ❖ Not all those you think of as friends are who they claim to be, nor do they all want what is best for you.

- ❖ **Iron sharpens iron so seek friends with strong characters.**

- You truly mean the world to your parents.

- Parents are exceedingly forgiving; however, it's ill-advised to push your luck.

- **Some parents can be controlling, manipulative, and uncompromising; therefore, learn to be bold but in a respectful way.**

- Send your parents a thank you e-mail, instant message, or letter occasionally.

- **Know that your journey may be different from what your parents have in mind; however, this is OK.**

- You should respect and follow your parents' household rules to a T.

- If you can't abide by your parents' rules and regulations, maybe it's time to move out.

❖ **Teach your friends to respect your parents' rules and regulations.**

❖ Knowing when to approach your parents is the difference between yes and no.

❖ Sneaking out of the house after your parents are asleep can be foolish.

❖ **READ WIKIPEDIA: "MURDER OF SHANDA SHARER"**

❖ Always let someone know your whereabouts.

❖ Under no circumstances should you get into a car with a stranger or someone you don't feel comfortable with.

❖ **READ WIKIPEDIA: "MURDER OF AMBER DUBOIS"**

❖ Make time to spend with your parents.

❖ Just because you are getting older doesn't mean your parents don't like having you around.

YOUNG PEOPLE | TEENAGERS

❖ The l9ttle voice inside is your best friend—get to know it.

- ❖ Try to be courteous to your parents regardless of how they treat you.

❖ Let your parents know you need parents and not friends during your developing years.

- ❖ Respect your parents, even if they don't respect themselves.

- ❖ If someone or something is bothering you, tell your parents or a responsible adult.

❖ Learn to verbalize your feelings and concerns because people are not psychic.

- ❖ You should never accompany an irresponsible parent to settle a score.

- ❖ Fundamentally, your parents want what they perceive to be best for you.

- Some parents will try to keep you dependent; however, seek independence.

- **Unfortunately, you might have to raise your parents.**

- Try to understand your parents' perspective.

- **Even though your parents may act perfect, they are just as imperfect as you are.**

- Avoid straying from the upright teachings of your parents.

- If someone touches you improperly, tell someone. If that person turns around and starts touching you improperly, call 911.

- **Committing suicide because you are being taunted due to your sexual orientation isn't going to resolve the situation.**

- If you are videotaped having homosexual or heterosexual sex and it goes viral, don't jump off a bridge. There's life after going viral.

- If you are gay, at least one of your parents might already know.

- **Give your parents time to absorb the news of your sexual orientation if they initially don't take it very well.**

- It's best to tell your parents about your sexual orientation rather than have them find out some other way.

- **You can't afford reckless friends, especially if you have more to lose than they have.**

- You won't understand some situations until you are much older.

- **There may be times when you will have to break the**

confidentiality of a friendship to get adult help.

- If your friend breaks the confidentiality of your friendship to get you help, you should thank him or her instead of resenting him or her.

- If you break the confidentiality of a friendship to get your friend help and he or she resents you and labels you a traitor, look at it this way: at least your friend is alive and you don't have to live with regret or remorse.

- **The best types of friends are the ones who do what is in your best interest regardless of the outcome for themselves.**

- Loitering after school—especially in a sketchy neighborhood—will inevitably get you in trouble.

- **FACT OF LIFE: SOME PARENTS HAVE A HARD TIME TELLING YOU JUST HOW PROUD THEY REALLY ARE OF YOU.**

YOUNG PEOPLE | TEENAGERS

- Learn not to be a people pleaser.

- **Avoid bad company or it will corrupt you—if not immediately, gradually.**

- You have nothing to prove to anyone but yourself.

- **If you don't know something, google it.**

- Pornography pollutes the mind and is hard to shake.

- **There are all sorts of weirdos lurking around the Internet; therefore, be wary and mindful of them.**

- Be careful not to post too much information about yourself or your family on the Internet.

- It's unproductive to go cruising around the Internet looking for a friend.

- **Be suspicious of people who send you ran4om friend requests.**

- ❖ Tell your friends about your Internet buddies.

- ❖ Never meet up with someone you met on the Internet.

- ❖ **Learn to be an asset to society rather than a liability.**

- ❖ Not everyone is like you, and that is perfectly OK.

- ❖ Not everyone will understand you, but don't let that prevent you from being yourself or make you a loner.

- ❖ **There will always be a teenager that is 16 & Pregnant; try really hard to not let it be you.**

- ❖ If your parents are still paying your bills, sex isn't for you.

- ❖ Sex is much more than a physical act.

- ❖ **Sex is for responsible adults who can afford daycare.**

- ❖ **Being a virgin at 21 is still respectable,**

regardless of what pop culture says.

❖ Do your best to be more progressive and better off than your parents.

❖ **Your parents did you a grave injustice if they taught you to hate a person based on his or her background, color, religion, sexuality, or age.**

❖ Your parents are not the ultimate killjoy; it's just that they are sometimes hypocritical in the way they parent.

❖ Ask your parents questions; however, if they refuse to answer, google it.

❖ **Learn to practice abstinence or safe sex.**

❖ Sexting is dangerous and could ruin future opportunities before you even know about them.

❖ **Once your nude pictures go viral, good luck in**

trying to get them removed from the Internet.

❖ If your nude pictures go viral, it is not the end of the world.

❖ Social media are fun, but be responsible.

❖ You are not a rotten child, and only a loser would say that to you.

❖ Dream, and dream *outrageously* big.

❖ Your dreams are insights into your destiny, and only you can bring them to fruition.

❖ Some parents do understand; they just act as if they do not.

❖ You are one of your parents' 99 problems.

❖ Stop wasting your time with reckless and senseless activities; instead, spend that time

doing productive and educational activities.

- It's unbeneficial to let video games or movies desensitize you to violence.

- Any kind of drug has the potential to be addictive.

❖ Pharm parties can get you hospitalized.

- Use your parents as an excuse to get out of bad situations.

❖ Texting and driving can be deadly.

- If you are drunk, call a sober adult to pick you up.

- It's better to call your parents to pick you up and be alive than to drive drunk.

- Drag racing is dangerous.

❖ Know your limitations.

- Stand up to and against peer pressure.

- You have to learn to be strong; if you are being bullied or cyberbullied, use that as an impetus to be the best you can be.

- **A bully is only as powerful as you make him or her.**

- At some point, you will have to stand up to the bully in your life—the sooner, the better.

- Bullies tend to harass people they are jealous of.

- Some hazing rituals can get you killed.

- **It's unwise to believe everything someone tells you; instead, be your own little Inspector Clouseau.**

- Just because someone is chronologically older doesn't mean he or she knows what is best for you.

- **Get into the habit of taking responsibility for your actions.**

- There's nothing you can't overcome—all you need are a beating heart and a sound mind.

❖ Learn to be determined to persevere.

- Cigarettes are addic20ive, and the earlier you start smoking them, the longer it will take to kick the habit.

- Eating is healthy, but overconsumption can lead to depression.

❖ Loving yourself is empowering; it's reckless to let anyone take that experience away from you.

❖ Education is a powerful and useful tool to counteract poverty.

- It's advantageous to know your family's history.

- It's a sad day when your parents are your pimp.

- ❖ **Be open to diversity, regardless of what people say.**

- ❖ Electronics are fun, but there's nothing like sitting underneath a mango tree to read a book.

- ❖ **Reading unlocks your imagination.**

- ❖ Get to know your parents on a deeper level; you will discover they are extremely cool people.

- ❖ **Your parents don't discipline you out of hate but rather out of love.**

- ❖ **Good or bad, one day you will understand why your parents raised you the way they did.**

- ❖ If your parents are abusing you, tell a responsible adult.

- ❖ You shouldn't be 16-years-old and weigh sixty-eight pounds, nor should you be 17 and weigh 220 pounds.

- ❖ **At some point in your life, you will have to teach your parents a thing or two about life.**

- ❖ Your parents are not only your teachers—some actually want to be students in your classroom.

- ❖ **Be a leader, not a follower; however, there will be times when you will have to follow in order to learn how to become an effective leader.**

- ❖ If you don't want to follow in the educational or professional footsteps of your parents, be honest with them as soon as possible.

- ❖ If your parents refuse to pay for your college education because you are not interested in the same career path as them, get a job and pay for it yourself.

- ❖ **There's nothing scarier to some parents than an independent child.**

- Parents will sometimes use their money to control you.

- You are not entitled to your parents' money.

- Parents fail at activities also—they just have the resources to cover up their tracks.

- **You and your parents are in the same boat concerning where your souls will end up–you can't save them, and they can't save you.**

- Your parents are not gods, so stop worshipping them.

- **Fight for your right to be you.**

- Learn what a budget is, and try to stick to one.

- Money doesn't grow on trees, so be smart when it comes to spending.

- **Your parents don't have to teach you about money in order for you to value it.**

- ❖ It's unwise to commit suicide because of your credit card debt.

- ❖ There's no such thing as free money.

- ❖ **Make plans for the future, write them down, and try to stick to them as best as possible.**

- ❖ Make plans for the future, write them down, and etch them in your memory, so the next time your so-called friend wants you to participate in illegal activities, you will remember those plans and the bright future you have ahead.

- ❖ The most successful people in life have plans.

- ❖ **The reason your parents divorced has more to do with them than you.**

- ❖ It's actually better that your parents got divorced.

- ❖ Your parents' divorce isn't an opportunity to milk them for all they are worth.

- ❖ **Stepparents can be extraordinarily sweet people; all you have to do is give them a chance.**

- ❖ Instead of financially depending on your parents, get a part-time job!

- ❖ **Instead of having sex after school, get a part-time job or participate in after-school activities.**

- ❖ If your part-time job is interfering with your schoolwork, get rid of it.

- ❖ **Working and making your own money gives you independence but not the authority to disrespect your parents.**

- ❖ Save most of the money from your part-time job to help pay for your college tuition.

- ❖ If you have a part-time job, contribute financially to your household.

- ❖ Spend your money wisely, and refrain from being a shopaholic.

- ❖ **Learn to be self-motivated and self-sufficient.**

- ❖ Show your parents you are trustworthy.

- ❖ If your parents go away on vacation, don't throw a crazy party and have hooligans destroy their home.

- ❖ **Your parents work hard to provide you with the finer things in life; appreciate that and teach your friends to do the same.**

- ❖ Trust and have faith in your parents.

- ❖ Pray for your parents.

- ❖ **Learn to think before you act.**

- ❖ Weigh the consequences of your actions before you act.

- ❖ To get yourself into trouble takes only seconds but to get yourself out of trouble can take years.

- ❖ **Just because you are young doesn't mean you are licensed to be irresponsible.**

- ❖ There's more to life than fancy cars, designer clothing, sex, drugs, and rock 'n' roll.

- ❖ Learn to appreciate the simple things in life; when you get older, you will be glad you did.

***
Young Ladies

- ❖ **MUSIC: "I HOPE YOU DANCE" BY LEE ANN WOMACK**

- ❖ **You are beautiful just the way you are; don't let anyone tell you otherwise.**

- ❖ If you are the only girl in your immediate family, you can't blame your parents for being overprotective.

- ❖ It's uncool to strive to be part of the mean girls' club.

- ❖ Some girls can be mean; don't pay any attention to them.

- ❖ **Stay focused on getting a good education instead of good sex.**

- ❖ Consistently assess your family's financial situation.

- ❖ **If your parents are struggling to make ends**

meet, the last thing you should be having is sex.

❖ Keep yourself occupied with after-school activities instead of boys.

❖ **Do homework after school instead of boys.**

❖ Most boys only want sex; and they genuinely don't know how to appreciate it until they are older, wiser, and more responsible.

❖ **Sending nude pictures of yourself to anyone is foolish.**

❖ **Failures are opportunities to learn something new about yourself.**

❖ Every female hates something about her body.

❖ **Being smart is fantastic; it's senseless to dumb yourself down to fit in.**

- Dumbing yourself down will eventually make you dumb.

- It's unwise to let your boyfriend convince you to participate in group sex with him and his friends.

- **Being promiscuous leads to a bad reputation.**

- If your boyfriend cheats on you with your best friend, that shouldn't be an opportunity to sleep with his best friend.

- **Absolutely no sex tapes, regardless of how much money you think you'll make from peddling them. Remember, a good reputation is priceless.**

- It's unwise to let anyone talk you into disobeying your parents' rules.

- **It's ill-advised to allow yourself to be pressured into sex, drugs, and/or drinking.**

- If you are raped, report your rapist—even if he is a family member.

- Most boys will say and possibly do whatever it takes to get into your pants.

- **Some boys will use your weaknesses and insecurities against you to get what they want.**

- Quit being pretentious and learn to accept yourself for who you *really* are.

- Puberty will hit you like a ton of bricks, so be prepared.

- **Your menstrual cramps will likely become less severe as you age.**

- What is a lovely teenager like you doing with a 36-year-old man?

- Some older men only like younger girls for one thing, and it's not your brain.

- **It's senseless to let anyone steal your youth.**

- You have your whole life to fall in love and have mind-blowing sex; it's foolish to rush the experience.

- **Love is a complex emotion.**

- **You will come to understand the real meaning of love over time and as you get older and hopefully wiser.**

- Banging your married teacher might be exhilarating but is dangerous.

- You are never too young to start planning for your future.

- Your parents know the trickery of most boys; hence, they are protective of you.

- **Parents usually know what is best for you.**

- Let your dad take you on your first date to show you how a man should treat a young lady.

- Keep family se3urity codes between you and your immediate family.

❖ **Your parents might nag you, but they mean well.**

❖ If your boyfriend doesn't respect your parents' rules, eventually he will not respect you either.

❖ **Just because your parents don't like your boyfriend doesn't mean you should fall truly, madly, deeply in love with him.**

❖ If you had consensual sex with your older boyfriend, it's unwise to let your parents talk you into calling it rape.

❖ **If you are underage and your parents hate your older boyfriend, it might turn out bad for him.**

❖ Know the meaning of statutory rape.

❖ If your parents don't like your boyfriend, it's usually for a good reason.

- ❖ **Learn to cook to maintain a healthy weight.**

- ❖ Practice healthy personal hygiene.

- ❖ **The clothes you wear to school should be the same clothes you have on at school.**

- ❖ Playing hooky from school is going to catch up to you.

- ❖ **Coitus interruptus (pulling out method) isn't the best form of birth control.**

- ❖ Sexually transmitted diseases (STDs) are still a reality.

- ❖ It's foolish to kid yourself; sex is oral, vaginal, or anal.

- ❖ **If you are offering it, boys will be lined up to get it with no commitment or responsibility attached.**

- Boys are almost entirely depending on you when it comes to birth control.

- **Most boys believe unplanned pregnancies are YOUR problem.**

- Seriously, can you afford to be 16 & Pregnant?

- **Some girls never bounce back from a teenage pregnancy.**

- If a boy likes you, he likes you—period.

- Pay more attention to a boy's actions than his words.

- **Having the right sense of self is tremendously powerful and very empowering.**

- No one will ever love you as much as you can love yourself.

- Sex isn't a requirement on prom night.

- ❖ **It's foolish to let a loser con you out of your virginity.**

  - ❖ If you are being mocked for being a virgin, no worries. At least, you never have to be concerned about morning-after pills or abortions.

  - ❖ Keep your sexual status private.

- ❖ **Learn not to make decisions based on emotions.**

  - ❖ Learn to control your emotions.

  - ❖ If your boyfriend dumps you because you don't want to have sex with him, be thankful.

- ❖ **MUSIC: "LET'S WAIT A WHILE" BY JANET JACKSON**

  - ❖ Date boys with potential and ambition.

- ❖ **It's not worthwhile to date rich boys merely because they are rich.**

- Don't let your rich boyfriend talk to you or treat you abusively.

- **Beware of fondling or girl-on-girl action at your all-girls' school.**

- Never leave home without money in your pocket.

- Don't let someone take you to a location where it will be difficult to get home on your own.

- **As you get older, you will hopefully meet men that are more refined.**

- Don't let a guy come between you and your best friend.

- A controlling boyfriend is dangerous.

- **If you and your boyfriend are beating each other up, you are in an unhealthy relationship; end it before someone is arrested.**

- Marriage is for adults.

- Stalking ex-boyfriends on Facebook and Twitter will only keep you entwined longer than need be.

- **Love and let go; if he doesn't want to be with you, let him go.**

- Don't let a guy keep stringing you along.

- Love is an adult emotion, so wait until you are older to be involved.

- **For most boys, sex is just that–sex.**

- Just because you are having sex with a boy doesn't mean he loves or even likes you.

- Boys think about sex differently than girls; for most, it's purely physical.

- **You will probably mature–both mentally and physically–earlier than your male counterparts.**

- You are not pregnant because he did not drink Mountain Dew that week!

- **One of your future goals should be to be an independent woman.**

- Just because your dad isn't in your life doesn't mean you can't have healthy relationships with men.

- There's no substitute for a father.

- Gravitating toward older men because your father isn't around can be a double-edged sword.

- **Learn to respect and value yourself; otherwise, no one else will.**

- If you lack respect for yourself, it's evident in the way you carry yourself.

- **Sit at the feet of mature and spiritual women and eagerly learn from them.**

- Even though you might think you know it all, there's so much you have no clue about.

- **Your mother might not be the best role model; however, there are other women who can fill her shoes.**

- At the end of the day, your biological parents are your parents—no matter what sort of relationship you had with them growing up.

- **Never be afraid to ask questions.**

- Don't let yourself to be talked into or out of an abortion.

- If you have a baby, he or she is primarily your responsibility, says the law.

- Nothing is wrong with being a God-fearing teenager.

- **Nothing is wrong with displaying a Godly character even if you are being mocked for it.**

- ❖ This isn't an advocation for masturbation; however, you have to get to know your body. At least once in your lifetime, drop a mirror on the floor, bend over it, and explore down there.

- ❖ There are three different openings down there: one for peeing, one for menstruating, and the other for pooping.

- ❖ **Enjoy your youth, but learn to make the right decisions as this could influence your life tremendously.**

* * *
Young Men

- ❖ You are a precious prince; act like it.

- ❖ **You are divinely blessed.**

- ❖ Learn to be a leader and not a follower.

- ❖ Don't let your peers talk you into doing sleazy things.

- ❖ **Know the difference between right and wrong, and act upon it.**

- ❖ Never hit a woman.

- ❖ All women should be respected even if they don't respect themselves.

- ❖ **Be wise about the men from whom you get advice about women.**

- ❖ **If you are in an abusive relationship, it's time to get adult help.**

- ❖ Just because a teammate is gay doesn't mean he's checking you out in the locker room.

- ❖ Don't let yourself become paranoid when surrounded by gay men.

- ❖ **If your coach or priest is hitting on or fondling you, tell an adult—no matter what the abuser says.**

- ❖ Using derogatory language toward a gay person is insensitive.

- ❖ Never participate in the thrashing of anyone.

- ❖ Never participate in group rape.

- ❖ **Be careful where you go and with whom.**

❖ READ WIKIPEDIA: "TYRONE BROWN"

❖ MOVIE: A BRONX TALE

- ❖ It's OK to cry.

- ❖ If you are hurt, it's OK to talk about your feelings.

- ❖ There's nothing wrong with feeling, but act on those feelings selectively.

- ❖ **If you are depressed or feeling suicidal, seek professional help.**

- ❖ Don't let yourself become desensitized to violence.

- ❖ Playing around with a loaded gun can get someone killed.

- ❖ **Don't take your father's gun to school to intimidate a bully.**

- ❖ Refrain from using money to impress girls; they should like you for who you are and not what you can buy them.

❖ **Sex isn't just an activity; it's a serious responsibility.**

❖ Just because your father isn't around doesn't mean you shouldn't know how to treat a girl respectfully on a first date.

❖ **Don't be too proud to ask for help if you need it.**

❖ As a teenager, you should be more focused on getting a good education than being the man of the house.

❖ As a teenager, it's not your responsibility to make sure your siblings have food to eat.

❖ **As a teenager, you shouldn't be shouldering your father's responsibility.**

❖ It's unbeneficial to allow yourself to be caught up in the drug game.

❖ **Once you allow yourself to become entangled in**

the drug world, it's difficult to simply walk away.

- It might be difficult to find a reputable mentor, but if you don't look for one, you won't find one.

- Be protective of the women in your life.

- Know the facts before defending the reputation of a girl.

❖ Allow yourself to grow into a honorable man.

- Always open the door for a woman.

- Never let a girl emasculate you.

- There's nothing wrong with loving a girl; however, it's foolish to let her use it to manipulate you.

❖ If you act like a punk, people will treat you like a punk.

- Enjoy your teenage years without doing foolish things.

- ❖ **Be rational instead of irrational.**

- ❖ There's nothing wrong with studying dance.

- ❖ Embrace your inner geek.

- ❖ **PEOPLE: MARK ZUCKERBERG**

- ❖ You might not get the girl today, but you never know what the future holds.

- ❖ If a girl doesn't like you because you are not fly enough, no worries. She isn't best for you anyway.

- ❖ **Even if she's lying next to you naked, no means no.**

- ❖ The reason your father isn't around has nothing to do with you.

- ❖ **You can still have an extraordinary life even though your father abandoned you.**

- There's no excuse for your father abandoning you.

- Being a responsible father is difficult for some men, so they don't even try.

- **Strive to be a better man than your father.**

- Some men are simply not good at following through; it's best not to grow into one of these men.

- Always remember what it felt like to grow up without a father, so when you have children, they never have to experience that feeling.

- **You have limitless potential.**

- Just because you grew up in the projects doesn't mean you can't grow out of the projects.

- **Never forget your roots.**

- Your past is your past; your future is much more important.

- **If you don't want to be a teenage father, practice abstinence or safe sex.**

- As a top-tier athlete, beware of gold diggers.

- It's unwise to become entangled with unsavory sport hustlers.

- **Be careful from whom you accept gifts because he or she might misinterpret the acceptance.**

- It's better to say no to gifts today and yes to a multimillion dollar National Basketball Association (NBA) or National Football League (NFL) contract tomorrow.

- **Instead of complaining about "the man," learn to be the man.**

- **Emulate the goodness in your father or other men.**

- Even though you are now a teenager, you should still let your mother hug you.

- **Just because your mother remarried or has a boyfriend doesn't mean you are not one of the main men in her life.**

- Teach your girlfriend to respect your parents.

- Instead of trying to control your girlfriend, accept her for who she is.

- **FACT OF LIFE: FRIENDS GROW APART.**

- Be careful whom you let into your inner circle as some people sense your potential and only want to drag you down with them.

- **Know when to let go of negative people.**

- No matter what society says, sleeping with numerous women is disgusting.

❖ READ: "THE 5 LOVE LANGUAGES: MEN'S EDITION" BY DR. GARY CHAPMAN

❖ Calling women *bitches* and *whores* is extremely disrespectful.

❖ Practice monogamy.

❖ **There will come a time when you will have to put away childish behaviors and hopefully this is before you start having sex.**

❖ It's unwise to let your father bully you into going to his alma mater.

❖ **At some point in your life, you will have to stand up to your father.**

❖ Financially invest in cultural events.

- ❖ **Keep a journal and write down your thoughts for clarity and release.**

- ❖ Develop strong relationships with other young men.

- ❖ Some adults—like coaches and priests—are predators and will use expensive gifts and make unrealistic promises to ensnare you into a sexual relationship.

- ❖ **If you find yourself sexually attracted to other boys, you might be gay.**

- ❖ Be a loyal and trustworthy friend.

- ❖ **Get to know yourself by spending time with yourself without masturbating.**

- ❖ No matter what your girlfriend says, always use protection.

- ❖ Take good care of your mind, body, and spirit.

- **Instead of spending hours in the gym exercising your muscles, how about spending a fraction of that time exercising your brain?**

- Girls love boys with a good sense of humor who also know how to dance and cook.

- **Accept and love yourself for who you are.**

- Getting a girl drunk so you can have sex with her can get you 5-10 years in jail.

- No matter how tough you think you are, prison will break you.

- **Just because your family is rich doesn't mean you shouldn't build your own empire.**

- Going to church and practicing Godly principles enriches your soul.

- ❖ **Refrain from sending nude pictures of your ex-girlfriend to the entire school, even if she cheated on you with your best friend.**

- ❖ It's distasteful to send pictures of your package to anyone.

- ❖ **Be responsible when it comes to social media.**

- ❖ So what—you are 18 and a virgin.

- ❖ If you no longer want to be in a monogamous relationship, tell the person instead of cheating on him or her.

- ❖ **Being honest with the girl you are in a relationship with can go a long way.**

- ❖ Have a clear idea of what you want—besides sex—out of a relationship before getting into one.

- ❖ **Always strive to be the best you can be.**

- It's pointless to waste your youth on smoking marijuana, playing video games all day, drinking, partying, and other foolishness.

- **Get yourself a part-time job if you find you have too much free time.**

- It's unwise to use money made from your part-time job to buy your girlfriend expensive gifts as this will leave you broke or buried in credit card debt. Your creditors will still have to be paid in the event she dumps you.

- **The devil does find work for idle hands.**

- Danger may lurk around any corner, so be prepared.

- Be responsible when it comes to money and don't use it to impress girls who will take it and then dump you when it's gone.

- **READ: "BEREOLAESQUE: THE CONTEMPORARY GENTLEMAN & ETIQUETTE BOOK FOR THE URBAN SOPHISTICATE" BY ENITAN O. BEREOLA II**

- Be inspired by other boys and learn to be an inspiration as well.

- **You never want to be known as the person always crying wolf, so choose your battles wisely.**

- If you make a sex tape with your girlfriend, by default, you should marry her.

- Making a sex tape with your girlfriend might initially seem like a good idea, but the consequences can be traumatic for her if it goes viral.

- **Tough circumstances can bring out the best or worst in you; the decision is yours.**

- Some girls are good for you, and others are no good. Know how to make that distinction.

- **Girls are fun, but it's absurd to let them distract you from your schoolwork.**

❖ The girls who disrespect you today might be the same girls chasing after you tomorrow.

❖ **No sex with your sister(s) or other family members.**

CHAPTER 2

PARENTING

***

Introduction

I'm not a parent but I figure being one has got to be one of the most fulfilling experiences of one's life. Even though there's no check for overtime and it will take a few years before the benefits kick in, to know that there's a little person who adores you has got to be a wonderful feeling.

When a child is born, he or she is depending on you to teach him or her how to become self-sufficient and to develop to his or her full potential.

It takes a lot for a child to one day grow to hate a parent, but that could have all been avoided had you prepared yourself before you made or accepted the sperm deposit.

Every person has the ability to be a good parent; it really depends on whether he or she wants to and are willing to take the necessary steps to ensure this.

I believe that in order to be a good parent all you have to do is remember what it was like being a child. I'm sure there were some things that your parents did right, some things they did wrong, and others they could have done better. All that happened to prepare you to one day become a parent. I'm sure being a parent isn't easy; however, it also doesn't have to be hard either.

Your children are biased when it comes to you. If you love and treat them fairly, you will never have to compete with anyone for their love and loyalty.

Remember what your parents did well and repeat it. Remember what they did badly and try not to repeat it, and in the midst of all that remembering, try to create some lasting memories for your children to one day emulate.

***
In General

- Being a parent is the most influential job you will ever have; hence, you should take it very seriously.

- **Children need structure, stability, discipline, your time, and most importantly your love.**

- It's unproductive to poison your children against certain family members because those family members might have to raise your children if you die.

- Make sure you appoint age-appropriate, responsible, and loving people—even if not biological family—to raise your children in case you die while they are still quite young.

- **If you don't want to be a parent, take necessary steps to prevent it.**

- No one can trap you into parenthood unless you participate in some way (except rape and incest victims).

- ❖ **Refrain from having children until you are emotionally stable.**

- ❖ Being an effective parent has more to do with your character than your finances.

- ❖ **Procreate only with someone who shares the same core values as you.**

- ❖ Have a clear vision of how you want your children to turn out.

- ❖ Having the right vision is crucial to raising children who will be assets to society.

- ❖ **It's not smart to go into parenting haphazardly.**

- ❖ If you can't love your children the way they deserved to be loved, give them to someone who can.

- ❖ **Just because you are not talking about incest, molestation, or sex doesn't mean it's not**

happening in your household.

❖ Your children might have come through you, but they belong to God.

❖ Give your child a name that will look good on a résumé or presid5ntial ticket regardless of how much money you have in the bank.

❖ No matter what your position in society is, your children need their *own* identity.

❖ Enjoy your children's early years because they go by quickly.

❖ You will never be a perfect parent; therefore, don't act like one.

❖ Take all the time needed to enjoy and to get to know your children.

❖ Make it a priority to know the whereabouts of your children.

- ❖ You had children; they did not have you.

- ❖ **Breaking the cycle of bad parenting in your family starts with you.**

- ❖ Children don't need cool parents; they need responsible ones.

- ❖ Your children need parents when they are developing and friends when they are developed.

- ❖ **Your child acts like an invalid because you treat him or her like one...**

- ❖ There are pros and cons when it comes to incentive parenting.

- ❖ **Let your children know who your enemies are because if your enemies can't get to you, they will settle for your children.**

- ❖ Be extremely transparent with your children.

- Instead of saying, "Do not," explain, "Why not."

- **Your children can be your greatest asset or your greatest liability.**

- As you require trust from your children, you should in turn trust them to make the right decisions.

- **Parents and child have a relationship; treat it as relationship rather than a dictatorship.**

- Just as you work diligently to improve professional relationships so, too, work to improve your relationship with your children.

- Just because you are older and taller doesn't mean you know everything.

- Allow your children to have *some* input.

- **It should be established from early on who the parents are.**

- Some children will run all over you if you let them.

- Spoiling your child is fine, but how will he or she survive in the real world, where people will not tolerate his or her entitled attitude?

- Let your children know that even though *you* love them and give them preferential treatment, not everyone will show them the same courtesy.

- **There's a reason your teenager doesn't listen or respond to you; consider your approach and tone.**

- Even though your children might not initially listen to your input and advice, still keep talking to them.

- Be open and honest with your children about your past drug and alcohol use and abuse.

- **Every now and again, sit your children down and explain your parenting style.**

- It's OK to not know the answer to every question.

❖ **Be open to input from other parents—including single people—about raising your children.**

❖ Not all advice about parenting is wise, so learn to be selective.

❖ It's inadvisable to let *your* parents or any other parents bully you into making decisions concerning your children that you don't feel comfortable with.

❖ **Be there for your children no matter what.**

❖ The environment in which you raise your children is extremely important.

❖ It's better to drive an American-made car and send your children to decent schools than drive a fancy foreign car and live in a bad neighborhood.

❖ **Get to know your children's friends; invite them over for dinner occasionally.**

❖ It's unproductive to let your children know which of their friends you don't like.

❖ To your children, you are their hero.

❖ You should never go to your children's school and fight the class bully.

❖ **Make it a priority to teach your children to be disciplined and self-controlled.**

❖ **As soon as your children become aware of money, teach them to value it.**

❖ If you don't teach your children about the pitfalls of credit card debt, the creditors will.

❖ **Keep your automated teller machine (ATM) receipts to yourself.**

❖ Teach and show your children how to live within their means.

- Never let your children know they have an inheritance coming their way.

- **Children primarily learn by example, so be a parent worthy of emulation.**

- It's more about what you do than what you say.

- **If your child is always sleeping and locked up in his or her room, they might be depressed.**

- Not all depression should be treated with pills.

- If your child must be on medication, monitor it carefully.

- **Learn to be an approachable parent; if not, you will miss what is really going on with your child.**

- Make time to hang out and be silly with your children.

- ❖ **Talk to your children about the dangers of drinking and driving.**

- ❖ Let your children know it's better to call you to pick them up than to drive drunk or tipsy.

- ❖ **You will have the most impact on your child from his or her birth to around age twelve; make those years count for something.**

- ❖ Teachers are there to educate your children, but not to take over your role as a parent.

- ❖ **You should hold your children accountable for disrespecting their teachers.**

- ❖ Visit your child's teachers regularly to develop a rapport with them.

- ❖ You and your child's teachers should be on the same page when it comes to disciplining your child.

❖ **Teach your children the most important fundamentals when they are young, and it will last a lifetime.**

❖ If you are a lukewarm Christian, don't be surprised if your children turn out to be the same.

❖ You have to be careful how you present religion to your children.

❖ **When it comes to teaching your children about your religion, you can't have a "do as I say but not as I do" attitude.**

❖ In order for your children to accept your religion, you have to live it.

❖ Even though people in your religion might have rubbed you the wrong way that is no excuse for abandoning God and teaching your children to do the same.

❖ **Just because you are a Christian doesn't mean**

your children will accept Christianity.

❖ You might be your child's biggest stumbling block in regard to spirituality.

❖ **If you consistently compromise your integrity, don't be surprised if your children do the same.**

❖ You shouldn't hold your children to higher moral standards than yourself.

❖ When your children are young, you have their attention; make it count for something.

❖ **Even though it might be humbling and difficult, admit and apologize if need be to your children when you have made a poor decision or acted inappropriately.**

❖ It's unfair to put your children in precarious situations where they might be forced to steal to survive.

- **Even though you are an adult and should know more, your children are very insightful, so listen to them.**

- Your children are your primary responsibility.

- When you find out that you are having a baby, make a decision that whatever you have you are going to take home.

- **The fundamentals of parenting have been the same forever.**

- Be conscientious about monitoring your child's activities on the Internet.

- **Avoid revealing personal details about your children via social media.**

- Refrain from using social media to punish or humiliate your children.

- Take numerous pictures of your children while they are growing up so you can remember how cute they were when they upset you.

- **It's not that your children are disappointing; it's that your expectations are unrealistic.**

- Under no circumstances should you allow your children to curse in your presence.

- **Raise your children to understand the concept of boundaries in relationships.**

- There will come a time when your children refuse to hang out with you; it's part of growing up.

- **Although you may be fine with your teenager having safe sex, you shouldn't allow him or her to have it ups2Oairs**

while you are downstairs cooking dinner.

- If the parents of your child's boyfriend or girlfriend forbid their relationship, you should respect that and not find a way to make it happen behind their backs.

- **Treat your children properly, and you can hope they will remember it when you are old.**

- Your child is your child whether he or she is gay or not.

- **Your love should be unconditional whether you agree or disagree with your child's lifestyle.**

- Supporting your children is different from agreeing with them.

- ❖ **If your children think you are a bum, they are probably right.**

- ❖ Pray for yourself and your children.

- ❖ **Ask God for guidance in raising your children.**

- ❖ You can't spiritually save your children.

- ❖ **You can learn many, many, many things from your children, but you have to sh2lt up and listen!**

- ❖ **You have to allow your children to fall on their faces and then learn to pick themselves back up.**

- ❖ Instead of telling your children not to play with fire, let the burn from the fire teach them.

- ❖ Your children can handle the truth; all you have to do is tell it to them.

- ❖ It's better to tell your children what is going on with you than to have them learn about it from outsiders.

- ❖ **Your children are profoundly impacted by your behavior both inside and outside the home.**

- ❖ You show your children what is important to you by the way you treat them.

- ❖ Expose your children to as many cultures as possible.

- ❖ **Teach your children to appreciate and respect other cultures.**

- ❖ There's a difference between appreciating and tolerating other cultures; teach your children the difference.

- ❖ Save up and take your family on international trips.

- ❖ **The lessons you teach your children will**

ultimately be your legacy.

❖ Children get their values and moral compass from you.

❖ **Children learn to respect themselves by watching you respect yourself.**

❖ Give your children someone to respect.

❖ Children know when they are being loved—they feel it.

❖ **Ideally, children should be invited into this world.**

❖ Your child isn't your personal punching bag.

❖ The emotional and physical abuse that your children experience during childhood can last a lifetime.

❖ Your children are not the reason you have a problem functioning in the real world.

- ❖ **Adopt a child only if you can love and treat him or her like your own.**

- ❖ Refrain from adopting a child for publicity; you might end up mistreating him or her.

- ❖ **Allow your children to live their own lives.**

- ❖ Snatch up your children before they officially cross over to the dark side.

- ❖ **Understand that your child's destiny might be different from the one you have in mind.**

- ❖ Teach your children to focus on and develop the inside rather than the outside.

- ❖ **Your child is looking to you for leadership and guidance—not for indignation and criticism.**

- Your children were not born racist; you probably had something to do with it.

- ### Racism is intolerable.

- There are some intangibles money just can't buy—like love.

- ### Every child needs to be acknowledged by both parents.

- Embrace new technology, as your children sure will.

- It's unwise to be left behind because of your unwillingness to embrace new technology.

- ### Your children need to feel wanted and needed, and only you can give them that.

- Children need the warmth and security of both mother and father.

- Disciplining your children is beneficial, but abusing them is destructive.

PARENTING

❖ **Children don't ask for much—just for you to be there.**

❖ The spirit of your child is extremely strong, but like glass, it too can break.

❖ **It's reckless to make excuses for your children's bad behavior; instead, try to correct it as soon as possible.**

❖ When your child becomes a teenager, that's really too late for discipline.

❖ If celebrities have more influence on your children than you do, you have a serious problem.

❖ Children don't need Louis Vuitton, Prada, or Versace merchandise; they just need nondesigner merchandise and you.

❖ **Wisely invest in your child's future instead of throwing him or her an exorbitant "Sweet 16" birthday party.**

- Address the problems in your child's life head on.

- Something might not be important to you, but it means the world to your child.

- **You complicate your relationship with your children when you try to live vicariously through them.**

- You had your life to live; now let your children live theirs.

- **As a parent, it's your responsibility to teach and show your children how to be strong.**

- If every time things get tough, you turn to the bottle, your child might develop the same destructive habit.

- **Resolve any issues with your children before they begin to hate you.**

- Whatever you invest into your children, you will reap.

- ❖ **Children are a return on investment.**

- ❖ It's unbeneficial to wait until you are on your deathbed before telling your children just how proud you are of them.

- ❖ **Trust your children as much as you want them to trust you.**

- ❖ Teach your children the importance of hard work.

- ❖ Raise pioneers, not squatters.

- ❖ Your money is your money; raise your children to make their own.

- ❖ **Encourage the inquisitiveness of your children.**

- ❖ Raise thinkers, not posturers.

- ❖ Whether you agree or disagree, you still have to respect your children's decisions.

- **One of the reasons your child might feel uncomfortable confiding in you is because, you have probably said, "I told you so" too often.**

- Communication is a two-way street.

- Communication involves more than you speaking and your child listening.

- **Learn to have dialogues instead of monologues with your children.**

- You might not have been the best parent during your child's developmental years; however, don't let him or her use that guilt to force you into making bad decisions now.

- **Parenting is an act of faithfulness.**

- Waiting until your teenage daughter is six months pregnant is way too late to start discussing sex.

❖ **Whether you are a Christian or non-Christian parent, you have to talk to your children about sex.**

❖ Do you want society to teach your children about sex?

❖ **Be mindful not only of your children, but of children in general.**

❖ The future of your children is intertwined with other children, so if their contemporaries are not doing well, neither are your children.

❖ Both boys and girls should have curfews.

❖ **As a parent, suicide shouldn't be an option.**

❖ If you kill yourself, you leave an air of despair over your children.

❖ **Teach your children to love people, inspire others, value life, and**

entertain those they love (L.IV.E.).

❖ You show your children how to overcome adversities by overcoming some yourself.

❖ **Show your children the importance of family by making yours a priority.**

❖ There's strength in showing your weaknesses to your children.

❖ It's uncool to magnify the weaknesses of your children in order to make yourself look good.

❖ **Have spirited family discussions as much as possible.**

❖ Have your children read aloud for thirty minutes, four times a week to develop their public speaking abilities.

❖ Teach your children to respect other people's things.

❖ When traveling with your children via public transportation, you are responsible for preventing them from tormenting other passengers.

❖ **If you are divorced, never talk trash about your ex-spouse in the presence of your children.**

❖ Let family members know that it's unacceptable to talk trash about your ex-partner in front of your children.

❖ **Your child has a divine purpose; stay out of its way.**

❖ It's no thoughtful to use guilt to get your children into or out of situations.

❖ **It's your responsibility to provide for the needs of all your children.**

❖ Children know when they are being bought.

❖ **Every child has a process he or she needs to go through; let it happen and stop interfering.**

- Be a spiritual person.

- **It's reckless to overwhelm your children with religion.**

- Work out your psychological issues before they overflow onto your children.

- **Treat your children the way you wanted to be treated when you were their age and in a similar situation.**

- You are your child's first love.

- There will come a time when your children will *stop* chasing after you.

- **Your relationship with your children is as complicated as you make it.**

- Achieve your primary goals before having children.

- Only hire babysitters who share your core values.

- ❖ It's unwise and emotionally unhealthy to keep your children isolated from society.

- ❖ **Teach your children to fish, and they will never go hungry.**

LESSONS FROM GENERATION X TO GENERATION NEXT

***
Mothers

- There's no other person as influential as you are.

- **It's a divine privilege to become a mother.**

- You don't have to physically give birth to be considered a mother.

- **You are equipped with everything you need to be an exceptional mother.**

- When you have a baby, you are the primary caregiver.

- Being a mother can sometimes be a daunting task, but you can do it.

- **You should grow with your children instead of just getting older with them.**

- Your children are a tremendous blessing.

- **It's not worthwhile to let your parents' bad parenting deter you from becoming a parent.**

- If you are struggling to raise one child, don't have any more babies unless you are in a solid marriage.

- **There's no such thing as part-time parenting; it's a full-time job with no overtime pay, and the benefits might take a while to kick in.**

- There's no me-time when you are a mother.

- No one can be a better parent to your child than you can.

- **Accept help and input on raising your children.**

- **You can never be the father your children need.**

- Even if you hate your children's father, they need to know who he is.

- **Just because your children's father no longer wants to be in a relationship with you doesn't mean you should keep him from them.**

- Love your children even if you don't like their father(s).

- **Show your children how to respect their father by doing so yourself.**

- If you deem your child's father to be poisonous, monitor his inte18actions with the child carefully.

- It's inadvisable to overcompensate with material items for your child's father absence from your child's life.

- **If you are having behavioral problems with your children, you only make a bad**

situation worse by dating someone they don't like.

- Refrain from putting your partner's needs ahead of your children's.

- It's unwise to bring strangers home to your children.

- **Your bedroom shouldn't be a revolving door.**

- If you want your daughter to be a virtuous woman, you will have to show her by being one yourself.

- **The true definition of a virtuous woman is <u>Proverbs 31:10–31</u>.**

- Your children shouldn't be worried about where their next meal is coming from.

- **While in school, your children should be focused on getting a good education, not worried about dinner.**

- Men come and go, but your children are forever.

- **It's not recommended to bring home or marry a young man to whom your teenage daughters might be attracted.**

- Being a cougar is overrated.

- Nothing is wrong with dating a younger man, but you have to be mindful of the role he will play in the lives of your children.

- **If your partner is looking lustfully at your daughter, get rid of him.**

- As a single mother naturally you want the companionship of man, but you have to be very careful who that man is.

- **Your home should be a sanctuary where your children feel safe and contented.**

- Your son also needs to be protected from your lovers.

- ❖ **Your son should never have to worry about protecting you from your drunken boyfriend.**

- ❖ Hug your son as much as possible, except in public, as he has a reputation to protect.

- ❖ Providing a secure home for your children should be more important than trying to find and keep a man.

- ❖ Breastfeeding is very healthy for babies, but might be considered
emotional abuse for a five-year-old.

- ❖ **It's unwise to let your mother overpower your decisions in terms of raising your children.**

- ❖ When the topic of sex comes up, use it as an opportunity to discuss it with your children.

- ❖ Do random checks on your teenage daughter to make sure she doesn't have a baby bump.

- **If your living environment is toxic, get out and take all your children with you. Never leave one behind.**

- No matter what you do, you can never force a man to love his children nor should you have to.

- **It's unwise to allow teenage lovers to shack up in your house.**

- There's nothing wrong with wanting to live your life, but as soon as you have children, it should stop being about *you* and instead be about *them*.

- Not to downgrade the importance of fathers, but as a single mother, you can do a heck of a job raising your children.

- **Your actions can make or break your children; unfortunately, you are that powerful.**

- To be an effective mother, you have to learn to balance discipline with love and tenderness.

***
Fathers

- **When God made you, he broke the mold; you are priceless and don't even know it.**

- Being a man means taking care of all your children, even the ones from wo13en you don't like.

- Having several children with different women is just downright sloppy.

- Just because you didn't grow up with a positive male role model doesn't mean you shouldn't get married first and then have children.

- **You don't have to be financially well-off to be an outstanding father.**

- There's more to being a father than your sperm donation.

- Fight as vigorously to be in your children's lives as you would for that six-figure job you crave so desperately.

- Never let anyone keep you away from your children.

❖ Your children think the world of you, even if they don't show it.

❖ **Even though you are a scumbag for the way you treat your children and their mother(s), there's still a window of opportunity to make things right.**

❖ Your children's mother should be the most important woman in your life unless you are married to another woman.

❖ **Always be respectful of your children's mother.**

❖ It's unbeneficial to use your children to spite their mother.

❖ Whatever is going on between you and your child's mother shouldn't have any impact on you being there for your child.

❖ **Do the decent thing and marry the mother of your children.**

- Children never forget the way you treat their mother.

- **It's unbeneficial to continuously pop by for sex with your children's mother and make no commitment—your children will not respect you.**

- You shouldn't only be a father to your biological children but also to those in need.

- Another man shouldn't be raising your children.

- **It's unbeneficial to be selfish; share yourself with your children.**

- It's not only a woman's job to raise children.

- What good are you to your family if you are locked up in jail?

- **Turn off Monday Night Football and hang out**

with your children.

❖ Give your children an opportunity to know you as a person and not just as someone who provides.

❖ **Get to know your children individually on a deeper level by spending quality with each of them.**

❖ Do you know if your children are being bullied? You will only find out if you talk to them.

❖ Take your children to cultural events.

❖ How does it feel to see another man taking care of your children?

❖ **READ WIKIPEDIA: "TEAM HOYT"**

❖ Stop being prideful and go see your children.

❖ **You might have been trapped into fatherhood, but the child isn't responsible.**

- Cry me a river because she trapped you; however, make sure you are on time to pick up your child and the child-support check is never late.

- **Your children need more than a child-support check; they need you.**

- Financially invest in your children instead of Hollister, Ralph Lauren, and Sean John.

- Be a hands-on father and change poopy diapers for both boys and girls.

- **You will never be the mother your children need.**

- Leave work early to surprise your children at school occasionally.

- If you have sons, take them on bonding excursions.

- **The pain of being abandoned as a child can last a lifetime.**

- Remember the pain you felt when your father walked out; that is the same pain your child is experiencing.

- Remember the faults of your father; try not to repeat them with your children.

- You should be the #1 man in your children's life.

- **If you treat your children well, there will be no competition for their love.**

- Your children are loyal to you; why are you not loyal to them?

- If you don't want a woman to have your child, you shouldn't sleep with her...period.

- **To your children, you are their Superman.**

- Give your children many hugs and even kisses.

- Show your son what it means to be a man.

- Be a humble father and get advice on raising your children.

❖ MUSIC: "BUTTERFLY KISSES" BY BOB CARLISLE

❖ A child's spirit is resilient but be very careful with it.

- ❖ Respect yourself and your body by not bringing different women around your children.

❖ If you think your child isn't paying attention to your lifestyle, you are kidding yourself.

- ❖ Treat sons and daughters impartially.
- ❖ If your children are not home at a reasonable time, go look for them!

❖ You might not be a celebrity, but your children are proud of you regardless.

- ❖ Your children should respect you as head of household.

- **To be taken seriously as head of household, you must act and behave accordingly.**

- If your children think your wife is head of household, it's completely your fault.

- **You should be the chief executive officer, your wife should be the chief operating officer, and both of you should act as chief financial officer.**

- You need a life insurance policy to make sure your family will not struggle if you die unexpectedly.

- Just because you didn't grow up with a positive male role model doesn't mean you can't be one for your children.

- **If you have children in different states by different women, make time for those children also.**

- It's foolish to abandon your children for the new chick in your life.

- Your children are your lifeline, both literally and figuratively.

- **If you think you have failed at being a responsible parent in the past, pick yourself up, dust yourself off, and try again before it's too late.**

- Let your children see you express emotions through laughing, crying, and praying.

- **If your daughter gets pregnant at sixteen, it's not worthwhile to say, "I would rather see you floating in the Mississippi than have an illegitimate child." That is a very cruel thing to say to a child.**

- If your daughter is raped, it's unbeneficial to say, "If you didn't dress like such a slut that would not have happened." She's already traumatized; that is the last thing she needs to hear from her father.

- **It's unproductive to be an overbearing dad.**

- Make your children feel important; if you do not, the wrong people will.

- It's foolish to leave the raising of your daughters to their mothers.

- **Be the first man to take your daughter on a date.**

- Tell your daughter to call you if her date asks her to pay for her meal.

- **Raise your daughters to be independent women, but still be respectful of the men in their lives.**

- Always make sure your daughters have available funds.

- Telling your sons it's OK to sleep around is bad parenting.

- ❖ **Take anger management classes instead of consistently blowing up at your children.**

- ❖ No sex with your daughters or stepdaughters.

- ❖ **Teach your sons about domestic violence.**

- ❖ Just because you gave up your dreams to start a family doesn't mean you should pressure your son to give up his dreams for yours.

- ❖ **MUSIC: "CAT'S IN THE CRADLE" BY HARRY CHAPIN**

CHAPTER 3

EDUCATION

Introduction

Getting a formal education was always a priority in my household. My parents believed that having a good education was something no one could ever take from you and as such was taken very seriously.

I spent most of my childhood in Jamaica, West Indies, and there were only three ways to be progressive: music, sports, or education. My parents chose to focus on education because for them this had a more lasting and beneficial effect.

I've always taken formal education very seriously but as I evolve as a person I've realized that there are other ways to educate oneself and not everyone belongs in a formal educational setting.

I do believe that children should be taught to be well-spoken, articulate, and cerebral, but I also believe that they should be taught to embrace the arts.

By no means am I in favor of children dropping out of school in ninth grade and running off to become rock stars; however, I'm in favor of expanding what's deemed educational.

If you love formal education then you should do your best to excel at it and the same should go for the arts.

If you believe in your heart that taking out $100,000 in

student loans to pay for college because your parents want you to become an engineer is futile then I think you should have a talk with your parents.

Education, whether formal or not, should be taken very seriously. Life ultimately is the best classroom but there are some things that must be learned in a formal setting.

EDUCATION

* * *

- **Use education as a tool to get out of an impoverished enviro14ment.**

- Knowledge is powerful if you make the right decisions.

- A good education is priceless.

- **A good education is something you'll always be able to take pride in.**

- Enjoy your school years, but take them very seriously because they go by so quickly.

- **Spend your time studying instead of playing video games and/or surfing the Internet.**

- Strive for more than a general education diploma (GED).

- In today's competitive workforce, a general education diploma (GED) will not get you very far.

- ❖ **Anyone can be good at school, but it takes hard work, discipline, and dedication.**

- ❖ Your parents want you to be the best student you can possibly be; hence, they are always on top of you when it comes to your studies.

- ❖ While still in high school, start scouting colleges and calculate how to pay their tuition costs.

- ❖ **Graduating from high school at sixteen is commendable.**

- ❖ Try not to be a high school or college drop out.

- ❖ Preparatory schools are not necessarily better than public schools.

- ❖ **While still in high school, apply for as many college scholarships as possible.**

- If you are invited to a college open house and have an irresponsible parent who has better things to do than take you there, still find a way to make it there.

- **Hang out with smart students and stay away from distracted ones.**

- Be aware of your credit card debt during your college years.

- If you don't have a multimillion-dollar job, you don't need to have twelve credit cards.

- **While in college, credit card companies want you, so they can sink their claws into your future.**

- Learn to balance school and play.

- **Ask your parents about their financial situation concerning your college ambitions.**

❖ Out-of-state tuition can wreak havoc on your parents' finances.

❖ **Your parents aren't obligated to pay for college.**

❖ If you can help with paying for your college tuition, do so!

❖ Just because your parents are paying for college doesn't mean you should be irresponsible and waste their money.

❖ **Try not to take semester-long breaks from your studies during your college career.**

❖ If you can, work to pay for college while in college.

❖ **Student loans are expensive and can suck the life out of your future.**

❖ Do your research when determining what type of student loans to apply for.

❖ Stick with government funded student loans instead of private loans.

- ❖ If you take out a student loan, take out only what you need.

- ❖ It's imprudent to take out a $100,000 student loan for a master's degree in dance unless you have a surefire way of making enough money to pay it back.

❖ Try to stick with in-state colleges.

- ❖ Ivy League colleges look great on résumés, but can you really afford them, and will they pay for themselves in the end?

❖ It doesn't matter where you went to school, your success will be determined by your drive, perseverance, and tenacity.

- ❖ College isn't for everyone, but you had better have a plan besides your parents' basement.

- ❖ If you are not going to graduate on time because you have been slacking off, tell your parents before they show up for graduation with the rest of the family.

- ❖ **If you are the first to graduate from college in your family, kudos to you.**

- ❖ Develop professional relationships with faculty and classmates, and keep in touch after graduation.

- ❖ Bond with, don't bang, your college professors.

- ❖ Have an after-college plan and work on it feverishly throughout your college years.

- ❖ **The college graduate with a plan gets the job.**

- ❖ Approach your teachers for recommendation letters before graduation.

- ❖ Always be on the lookout for potential job opportunities.

- ❖ **If you work while in college, be careful not to let anyone convince you**

to quit college for a less-than-stellar job.

- It's inadvisable to allow your current job to distract you from finishing college.

- **Under no circumstances should you quit your full-time job for a nonpaying internship.**

- As you get older, it will be more difficult to go back to school.

- **It's never too late to return to college to complete your degree.**

- Get your formal education out of the way as soon as possible so you can get on with your life.

- **Just because you already graduated from college doesn't mean you can't take a few classes to improve your marketability.**

❖ **VISIT: WWW.LUMOSITY.COM**

❖ It's best to get your formal education out of the way before getting married and starting to have children.

❖ Even if you have a learning disability, you can still be a prosperous pupil.

❖ Cheating is a temporary fix to an ongoing situation.

❖ **Invest in a semester-abroad program.**

❖ It's pointless to waste your college years being a drunken party animal.

❖ **If you are on a scholarship, you can't afford to cut classes and get bad grades. There will be lots of time to party after college when you have more income. Now is the time to be disciplined and focused.**

❖ If you are in your final year of law school and meet an athlete or entertainer, it's inadvisable to quit school to follow him or her around the country or world unless there's a marriage certificate with both your names on it and a sweet prenuptial agreement.

❖ Just because you are heading to the National Basketball Association (NBA) or National Football League (NFL) doesn't mean you shouldn't be an intellectual.

❖ **Allow yourself at least two years of college before signing up for the National Basketball Association (NBA) or National Football League (NFL) draft so you can develop mentally and socially.**

CHAPTER 4

CAREER

* * *

Introduction

I've stumbled more in my professional life than I'm willing to admit but since we're all friends here, I feel compelled to share.

I spent my late teens and early twenties working in retail, but I always had a feeling that that wasn't for me. I told myself that I was just passing through.

After I graduated college, I dumped my retail job expeditiously and became an administrative assistant but I always knew that wasn't for me either.

I went back to school for television and broadcasting and thought I could get used to this. After that experience, I got an internship and was later hired as a contract worker, but I screwed that up by plagiarizing. Even though I liked broadcasting, I didn't like what I was doing, so instead of quitting, I sabotaged myself. I revealed my duplicity to my direct report and quit. To date, that is my most haunting professional experience.

After that humiliating experience, I went back to administrative work. I'm currently an executive assistant, but I know that's not where I'm meant to be.

Throughout my professional life, I've learned many things—all of which are on the following pages—but one of the most significant is that you have to decide early on what it is you want to do professionally and don't suppress it.

I believe that dreams are insights to our destinies, and if you keep dreaming about a certain profession, you should at least make an effort to pursue it.

Once I had a boss who wanted to be pianist but his parents told him that he was going to be a lawyer. He did as they suggested and is a pretty good lawyer, but I remember speaking to him about his career path and I could tell that there were definitely times when he wondered to himself about what could have been.

Trust me; you don't want to be the person who wonders about what could have been.

In hindsight, I've always known that a project like this was my calling, but like most people I suppressed it.

I do believe that even though we sometimes lose our way, God has a way of bringing opportunities back around.

I encourage you to be bold and do what you know deep down in your heart you were born to do.

***
In General

- **Always think in terms of a career (long term) rather than a job (short term).**

- Take online personality tests to determine which career would be suitable for you.

- Before going on a job interview, do extensive research about the company.

- **When you go for a job interview, be sure to pay attention to the atmosphere of the company.**

- Know which questions are appropriate and inappropriate for prospective employers to ask during an interview.

- Even though you are the one being interviewed, don't be afraid to question your interviewer.

- Jobs come and go, but careers are more calculated.

❖ It's never too late to switch careers.

❖ You shouldn't let anyone pressure you into choosing a certain field.

❖ It's not recommended to ignore your parents' input when it comes to a career, only to sponge off them later.

❖ Be pragmatic when choosing a career.

❖ Be bold and make your own decisions in terms of a career.

❖ Choose a career that brings you personal fulfillment rather than financial gain.

❖ A career with heart helps to refine your character.

❖ It sucks to be rich and hollow.

❖ It might take a while to find your professional

niche, but don't give up.

- When you are single, it's advantageous to experiment with different fields; however, as soon as you start a family, it's time to settle down.

- Just because you didn't go to an Ivy League college doesn't mean you can't compete with those who did.

It's unbeneficial to allow yourself to be pushed around by Ivy League graduates; you deserve to work for the company as much as they do.

- It's imprudent to look down on graduates who did not attend Ivy League colleges.

Your work should be filled with integrity.

- If you don't like your job, quit instead of sabotaging yourself.

- In order to get your dream job, you should first have an idea of what it is.

- **If you are passionate about your career, the money will come eventually.**

- In your twenties, you shouldn't spend more than two years with a company.

- In your twenties, it's advantageous to experiment in different fields. However, in your thirties, it's time to get serious and choose one.

- **Do what you are supposed to do at work and let God cover your tush.**

- Know your strengths and weaknesses, as this will keep you from having a boring, dead-end job.

- When you go to work in the morning, you should feel as if you are going to adult playtime.

- **When you do find your dream career, be determined not to let it consume your life.**

- There's a difference between doing a fantastic job and overcompensating.

- **Learn to enjoy and have fun with your coworkers but within boundaries.**

- Boundaries are essential at the workplace.

- Lack of boundaries at the office sometimes causes major blowouts.

- **Get a feeling for your coworkers' personalities and beliefs before you start cracking jokes.**

- Know which coworkers are cool and which ones are uncool.

- Be mindful of cultural differences at the office.

- Strive to maintain professionalism even though you hate your job.

- Work as if you are working for God and not for a company.

- ❖ **The work environment can be negative at times; do your best to stay positive.**

- ❖ Learn to make the best of any negative work situation; it will make you a better person in the end.

- ❖ A difficult boss can make or break you—the decision is yours.

- ❖ It's reckless to quit your job unless you won the lottery or have a better one lined up.

- ❖ **As a boss or supervisor, you should be positive and inspiring.**

- ❖ **If your boss or supervisor isn't inspiring, learn to inspire yourself.**

- ❖ When submitting a picture of yourself to an employer, make sure it's one that is professional and not one with you in your skivvies or partying.

- Always maintain a professional personal e-mail address, instead of one like hotpantsusa@gmail.com.

- **Nepotism and favoritism are unpleasant realities in the workplace; deal with it.**

- Nepotism isn't usually beneficial to the person who receives it because it doesn't help to develop character.

- Nepotism is the beginning, but you determine the ending.

- **Just because you are an high level executive doesn't mean you should be an A-level douche bag.**

- It's wise and advantageous to align yourself with people who are going places professionally.

- The workplace isn't the place for your political agenda.

- **Regardless of your political views, don't bombard your coworkers with them.**

- Whether you like your job or not, you still have student loans and credit card debts to pay off, so get on with the business of making money.

- **Plan to work hard when you are young, so you can enjoy the fruits of your labor when you are older.**

- Practice working hard and smart.

- No matter what anyone says, hard work does pay off...eventually.

- **If you love your career, you are blessed and should thank the heavens above.**

- Have you ever thought of entrepreneurship?

- E-mails can be used to prosecute you, so be careful what you write.

- **Even if you delete an e-mail; it's still**

somewhere in the virtual abyss.

❖ Never respond to e-mails while you are upset.

❖ **Keep all your follow-up e-mails just in case your unscrupulous boss throws you to the wolves.**

❖ Sometimes it's unwise to work for a friend.

❖ **Sometimes working for a friend can hinder your personal and professional development.**

❖ If you were hired by your best friend from a previous job, your interaction at the office should be professional regardless.

❖ **It's unfair to fire a hard-working employee to make room for your slacker son.**

- When you are doing what you are born to do, it doesn't feel like work.

- **It's inadvisable to be afraid to rock the boat even if you are part of the minority.**

- Don't let your work performance deteriorate because of a crappy work situation.

- Never let your jerky boss bring you to the brink of tears, and if you feel the tears welling up in your eyes, excuse yourself and run to the restroom to let it out.

- **When you are feeling too comfortable on the job, it's time for new challenges.**

- You will never be adequately compensated unless you are working for yourself.

- Careers in technology are extremely promising.

- **For your company to remain competitive,**

innovation and evolution are necessary.

- Douche bags are in every company, and you might be one.

- Working for companies with international locations can be advantageous for your career development.

- **Try to work for a company with a diverse board of directors and management team; if they all look the same, that could be a problem.**

- **Some company functions are like congressional hearing, they are simply for posturing.**

- No job situation is ideal, even if you are the boss.

- Avoid any participation in cover-ups because the one lowest on the totem pole is usually thrown to the wolves first.

- ❖ **Your job isn't the best place to look for a new sex partner.**

  - ❖ Sex between coworkers is insane both literally and figuratively.

  - ❖ No sex in the copy room after hours—take that lust offsite.

- ❖ **Discussing deeply personal sexual topics at work is unprofessional and icky no matter the work environment.**

  - ❖ Gossiping will get you in trouble or fired.

  - ❖ Don't be fooled, supervisors know who the gossipmongers and troublemakers are.

- ❖ **If you work closely with high level executives, learn to keep your mouth shut in regard to the kind of person he/she really is.**

CAREER

- If you know that high level executives are fudging financial reports, you have a moral dilemma on your hands.

- **Never talk trash about anyone from the office with anyone from the office.**

- It's good to hang out with coworkers after work, but keep in mind that you will see them at work tomorrow.

- **Try to live in harmony as best as you can with your coworkers.**

- Just because your boss left the company doesn't mean you should follow him or her to the new company.

- **Learn to make the right professional decisions for yourself independent of your mentor.**

- If you and your husband or wife are into freaky activities, keep them away from your place of employment.

❖ As an executive, you shouldn't be banging the interns.

❖ If you have a mister or mistress, your executive assistant shouldn't be assisting him or her.

❖ If you have a mister or mistress at your place of employment, you shouldn't be parading him or her around the office.

❖ It's usually obvious whom the boss is banging because that person typically walks around as if he or she is untouchable.

❖ It's great to be cool with the boss, but it's unwise to braggadocios about it.

❖ The business world is very fickle; know this before you become involved in the debauchery.

❖ In business, it's just business—nothing is personal (yeah right).

❖ Your best friends who lack business shrewdness shouldn't

be your business partners.

❖ Try not to mix business with pleasure; that is to say, refrain from getting former lovers hired at your company.

❖ Avoid hiring family members or friends who might bring your dirty laundry to work.

❖ **There's something to be said for compartmentalizing your life. You shouldn't mix your professional life with your personal life.**

❖ Avoid giving salacious details at work about the mind-blowing sex you had last night.

❖ Be nice to your assistant; after all, she does book your travel.

❖ **If you have an assistant, it's impossible for her to do a good job without lack of direction,**

respect, and communication from you.

- Undermining your subordinates can prove to be regrettable for you.

- Your boss might act like God, but you know better.

- Always be open to learning new skills.

- **Apply specific, measurable, attainable, realistic, and timely (SMART) tactics not only to your job, but also to your life.**

- To flesh out and execute any task, you need to ask, who, what, where, when, and why.

- **You can become an asset to your organization if you are an outstanding public speaker who knows how to connect with any audience.**

- Take speech classes to enhance your marketability.

- Always use visuals to capture and engage your audience during presentations.

- **When it comes to visual presentations, there's no need for convoluted PowerPoint decks; instead, keep it short and flowing.**

- There's a time and a place for everything, but your job isn't the place to show off your physical assets.

- **Men are easily distracted by visuals; help them out by dressing discreetly for work.**

- Yes, most men still make more money than their female counterparts do; however, women are catching up.

- Always keep your options open.

- ❖ **It's never too late to step out on faith with trying a new career.**

- ❖ You don't want to be known as a jack of all trades but master of none.

- ❖ **Balance between personal and professional life is necessary for your career to thrive.**

- ❖ As a woman, you can have a successful career and a healthy family life.

- ❖ **It's unwise for you as a woman to lose your warmth in the frostiness of the business world.**

- ❖ Women executives can be just as callous and calculating as their male counterparts.

- ❖ Women can play ball too; all they need is an invitation onto the field.

- **You will sometimes have to create your own opportunities within your company.**

- Challenge yourself consistently with new assignments.

- **It's inadvisable to make enemies where you can't make friends.**

- Always have a go-to friend at the office.

- Learn to be adapt1ble to change; this will add to your value.

- **You never know when you might need a reference, so try to maintain at least three healthy professional relationships at your current job.**

- Try to leave your job on favorable terms.

- There will be politics at work; do your best not to be caught up in it.

- **If your job is a certified graveyard, resurrect yourself out of there as soon as possible.**

- You know you are in the wrong profession if you constantly think about going postal.

- At the office, some people genuinely want to know what is going on to fix the problem while others just want to know for gossiping purposes. Know whom to trust and whom not to trust.

- **It's not recommended to let complacency keep you in mediocrity.**

- Some supervisors are extortionists; it's up to you if you participate in their schemes.

- **It's better to perform your daily activities slow and accurately than fast and inaccurately.**

***
Employees

- **Always be grateful for your job, even if it sucks.**

  - Even if your current job isn't your dream job, you still have to respect it.

  - Hate your job? Join the club or do something about it.

  - No job is forever—thank God.

- **Know what is going on with your company by consistently checking the blogosphere.**

  - Know when to jump ship before it sinks with you aboard.

- **No matter what your employer says, you are on a need-to-know basis.**

  - Whispering behind closed doors is never good.

- Be mindful of management shake-ups and what they mean for you.

- **If you are in a good professional situation, it's unwise to abuse it.**

- It's great if you are allowed to work from home, but it's imprudent to exploit it.

- At work, you are part of a team whether you like it or not.

- As a sexy chick you should not let yourself to be conned into sleeping with your boss for a promotion.

- Use your head instead of giving head at the office.

- **If the Federal Bureau of Investigation (FBI) is sniffing around, something odious is going on.**

- Be loyal to yourself first and then to your employer.

- There's nothing wrong with admiring your boss, but it's not recommended to be hypnotized by him or her.

- Be careful whom you choose as your mentor during your professional years.

- **No boss or organization is infallible.**

- Just because your boss is as sweet as cherry pie doesn't mean you should take advantage of him or her.

- Have s5x with your boss at your own risk.

- **Not all that glitters is gold—some of it's actually stolen or on a credit card.**

- Some employers are doing the best they can, so be patient with them.

- **If your boss asks, implies, or tells you to shred confidential papers, call the Federal Bureau of Investigation (FBI) immediately.**

- Shredding, deleting, or destroying evidence on behalf of your employer is illegal.

- Releasing confidential documents to the media about your employer is unforgivable unless your employer is a crook.

- **Potential employers investigate you via social media, so clean up your profile b5fore applying for a job.**

- Your Facebook page is *really* what is keeping you from that corner office.

- **READ: "DON'T SWEAT THE SMALL STUFF" BY RICHARD CARLSON**

- If you have an itchy Twitter finger, create an anonymous account. Then you can say whatever you want, whenever you want about whomever you want.

- **PLEASE NOTE: THE BIG SHOTS ARE THE ONES WHO SCREW UP THE COMPANY, BUT THE UNDERLINGS ARE USUALLY THE FIRST TO BE LAID OFF OR FIRED.**

- Learn to be tactful when it comes to sensitive information.

❖ **Being diplomatic will add longevity to your career.**

- ❖ Try to be Switzerland in all professional conversations.

- ❖ Study your boss, as this will help you to better communicate with him or her.

- ❖ Even if you consider your boss to be dumb as rocks you still need to respect him or her.

❖ **Always have a backup plan in case you are laid off or fired.**

- ❖ Most of the time, being laid off has more to do with your company than with you.

❖ **If you have been laid off, stop mentally torturing yourself wondering what you could have done better and make the best of this time.**

- ❖ Know your rights as an employee.

- ❖ It is unbeneficial to allow yourself to be intimidated by your employer.

- ❖ **Some unions tend to be like the US government; they are usually working both sides.**

- ❖ Strive to be on point in all situations where your supervisor is present, even at the Christmas party.

- ❖ Respect in the workplace must be earned, not demanded.

- ❖ **Even if you think your boos thinks you are dumb as rocks, don't be afraid to ask questions, even the ones you think might be irrelevant.**

- ❖ Check your paycheck stubs consistently.

- ❖ Be wary of companies that want to pay you by personal check rather than official company checks.

- ❖ Just because you have worked for a company for twelve years doesn't mean it is dedicated to you.

❖ Be a reliable and trustworthy employee.

❖ **Always look for ways to improve your company's reputation in the marketplace.**

❖ Sporadically, check out your company's rating with the Better Business Bureau (BBB).

❖ Make sure you are being adequately compensated for your hard work because ain't nothing going on but the rent.

❖ **Know and value your worth.**

❖ If you let your employer use and abuse you, you have no one to blame but yourself.

❖ Spend more time doing the actual work than kissing up to your boss.

❖ **It's inadvisable to badmouth your employer to new employees.**

❖ Always leave your crackberry at home while on vacation.

- **It is unwise to overwork yourself because when you kick the bucket, some employers will step over your dead body and continue on to the new recruit before you make it to the morgue.**

- Taking work home consistently can and sometimes does ruin personal relationships.

- Discussing work at home is fine, but it's foolish to become fixated on it.

- **As a woman, learn how to negotiate and play hardball.**

- Be nice to the service people in your building.

- Know who the key people in your organization are, and know their backgrounds.

- **Stay focused on becoming an invaluable employee, knowing that**

you might not always be recognized for it.

❖ Do your best to always make your boss look good.

❖ **Try not to burn any bridges because you never know what the future holds.**

❖ Having a good supervisor is extremely beneficial and very rare. Learn to appreciate him or her.

❖ **Always take the initiative.**

❖ Your boss doesn't expect you to be like other employees; however, he or she does expect you to put your best foot forward.

❖ **Some employers genuinely care about you and your career development.**

❖ Take advantage of your company's tuition reimbursement policy.

- ❖ **Make sure your friends or acquaintances are carefully vetted before you submit their résumés to your Human Resources Department.**

- ❖ Go to work every day with a hopeful attitude.

- ❖ It's not nice to invade a coworker's space with your crap.

- ❖ **DOCUMENTARY: <u>ENRON: SMARTEST GUYS IN THE ROOM</u> (2005)**

- ❖ Sometimes being fired can be the best thing that ever happened to your mediocre career.

- ❖ It's imprudent to allow yourself to be trapped in a job or career.

- ❖ On your job, you will sometimes have to learn to be iron like a lion in Zion.

- ❖ **READ: <u>CONFESSIONS OF AN S.O.B.</u> BY ALLEN NEUHARTH**

***
Employers

- **Value and appreciate your employees.**

  - Consistently reiterate to your employees how valuable they are to your organization but don't only tell them—implement programs that show them.

- **Good employees are priceless and hard to come by.**

  - Listen to and apply employee suggestions.

  - Treat your employees as you would want to be treated if you were in their positions.

- **Stay away from your employees' 401(k) accounts and don't invest funds unwisely.**

  - Think of your employees and their families before making reckless executive decisions.

❖ **Bargain with your own money instead of your employees' payroll.**

❖ Employees should have all they need, most of what they want, with some freebies in between.

❖ It takes just one loser on the Board of Directors to ruin your company.

❖ **It's unbeneficial to miss out on wonderful employees because of one high level jerk.**

❖ Supervisors shouldn't be allowed to terrorize their subordinates without consequences.

❖ Subordinates shouldn't be allowed to disrespect supervisors without consequences.

❖ **It's irresponsible when a company is begging the government for funds for the former chief executive officer to walk away with a $75**

million severance package.

- ❖ **It's cost-effective to retain quality employees.**

- ❖ As a supervisor, having office favorites is fine as long as it doesn't interfere with your decision making.

- ❖ **If you can't afford to pay your interns at least treat them like human beings.**

- ❖ Interns should be taught valuable business and life lessons that will be beneficial to their futures.

- ❖ **Having a sexual relationship with a subordinate is risky.**

- ❖ Have fun with your employees.

- ❖ **HOTSHOT COMPANY: GOOGLE**

- ❖ Invest in five summer Fridays annually.

- Treat your employees with dignity, and they will remember it when you fall on hard times.

- **Without good employees, your company isn't worth anything.**

- Invest in tuition reimbursement and training programs.

- **It's unpleasant to be a scrooge to the service people in your building during the holiday season.**

- All personal information about employees should be kept strictly confidential.

- **You will never make all your employees happy, but strive for at least 85 percent.**

- Discriminating against a candidate based on his or her name is illegal.

- The chief executive officer sets the tone of the company.

- ❖ **It's OK to let employees work from home periodically.**

- ❖ Embarrassing employees in front of the entire company is rude.

- ❖ There are more productive ways of teaching promptness than having tardy employees sing, "I'm a little teapot."

- ❖ **The office should have heat in the winter and air conditioning in the summer.**

- ❖ Encourage volunteer activities among team members.

- ❖ **Giving bad references about good former employees is wrong on many levels.**

- ❖ Acknowledge employees for their achievements in the moment.

- ❖ **Offer employees the option of transferring to other**

departments—within the company—if they are unhappy in their current department.

- Having a Wii console in the break room isn't a bad idea.

- Invest in an Automated External Defibrillator (AED).

- **Abide by the employment laws of your country.**

- Pay attention to who is *doing* whom.

- **Sexual harassment claims should be taken very seriously.**

- Creating and enforcing an appropriate dress code is crucial.

- Excessive spending on unnecessary technology is a waste of money.

- **Instead of squandering millions on items the**

company doesn't need, how about giving your employees a sizeable pay raise?

❖ Bagel Mondays and Pizza Fr9days are not going to break the bank.

❖ Invest in a people-friendly receptionist.

❖ **Spend the time and money needed to train your management team, so they know how to manage effectively.**

❖ Just because someone is a supervisor doesn't mean he or she knows how to be a good or effective team leader.

❖ **Investing in a corporate consultant could be beneficial to your organization.**

❖ High turnover reflects badly on your company.

- ❖ **Poll your employees every six months to see how you are doing as an employer, but only if you care.**

- ❖ Allow employees the freedom to be open and honest without fear of retaliation.

- ❖ Always look for ways to improve the office environment and culture.

- ❖ **It's inadvisable to treat your customers better than your employees.**

- ❖ Stifling the growth of deserving employees stifles the company's growth.

- ❖ **Documentation without implementation is futile.**

- ❖ Study other companies to see what makes them such a hit with their employees and try to incorporate some of those strategies.

- Visit blogs to see what employees are saying about your company.

- **Know the strengths and weaknesses of your employees.**

- Biweekly compensation might be suitable for the company but is difficult for many people receiving it.

- **Christmas or holiday parties should be in December; no one wants to go to one in January or February.**

- There should be an open bar at the Christmas or holiday party.

- **Bonuses should be paid out in December.**

- If you are not handing out bonuses, let your employees know beforehand.

- Emplo25ees shouldn't be the last to know if you are selling the company.

❖ **What is the purpose of an exit interview if you are not going to do anything about the complaints received?**

❖ Invest in a solid and thorough Human Resources Department.

❖ **The head of your Human Resources Department should be able to pull any executive aside to reprimand him or her for unsavory behavior.**

❖ Employees should have enough faith in their Human Resources Department to feel confident that any issues they have with supervisors or executives will be addressed and dealt with impartially.

❖ **It says a lot about your company if your Human Resources Department is one of the weakest**

departments in your company.

- Unfortunately, some companies don't pay attention to the foolishness of their supervisors or executives until they fire the wrong person and are then sued.

❖ As an employer, you should practice effective communication.

- As an employer, it's your responsibility to enforce and monitor boundaries between supervisors and subordinates.

CHAPTER 5

HEALTH

* * *
Introduction

My weight has been a rollercoaster ride. Over the years, my weight has fluctuated like the US stock market and for as long as I can remember it has always been this way. Like most issues we struggle with, this one stemmed from my childhood years.

When I was growing up, my parents did their best to make sure we always had something to eat but there were times when I craved more food, not because I was greedy but because I was still hungry. I ate what was given to me and didn't complain.

When I began high school, we had a health class that focused on teaching us healthy eating habits. But what happens during high school? Puberty. Puberty hit me like a ton of bricks and emotionally threw me for a loop.

At one point in my teenage years, I would unbeknownst to my brother compete with him. If he could eat it, I could eat it too; however, he was a boy who worked out or participated in sports every day while I sat home and watched *General Hospital*.

Currently, I need to lose like eighty-five pounds (I'm not massive); I feel uncomfortable and miss my smaller frame. What I've learned so far on this weight journey of mine is that health is more than physical, it's also mental. Truth be told, I have spent years mentally torturing myself but on the outside I looked good.

To be truly healthy, you have to pay attention not only to the physical but also your mental well-being, which honestly is more important. Your mental state of mind dictates which direction your body moves.

* * *

- **Learn healthy eating habits as soon as possible.**

  - Get help if you are having difficulties losing weight.

  - Losing weight will take time, so be patient.

  - Ask for input before deciding to lose weight.

- **No matter how strong you think you are, your body is very fragile.**

  - Consistently abusing your body will inevitably take its toll.

  - Know your body mass index (BMI).

- **DOCUMENTARY: SUPERSIZE ME (2004)**

  - Get to know and love your body.

  - Your body is different from everyone else's, but that is perfectly OK.

- **Mix up your exercise routine as this will help with motivation and consistency.**

  - Exercise for at least thirty minutes a day, four times a week.

  - Working out at the gym isn't the only way to lose weight.

  - The gym is for exercise, not sexercise.

- **If your health insurance offers a gym membership reimbursement plan, take full advantage of it.**

  - Enjoy food but avoid overindulging.

- **Make time for annual checkups.**

  - If you feel pain, your body is trying to get your attention; it's unwise to ignore the feeling.

- **Some say, "Pain is weakness leaving the**

body," but sometimes it's the body acknowledging its weakness.

❖ Consistently drink lots and lots of water.

❖ **Lose weight for you—not for anyone else.**

❖ It's better to lose one hundred pounds in two years than in six months.

❖ It's unproductive to let anyone make you feel uncomfortable about your weight.

❖ **Know your family's health history.**

❖ Too much sugar and salt is unhealthy.

❖ **Studies have consistently proven that eating fruits and vegetables helps individuals maintain a healthy weight.**

- Have a list of questions to ask your doctor at every visit, and don't leave until they are answered to your satisfaction.

- Switch doctors if you don't feel comfortable with the one you have.

- **Google your doctors periodically to see what is being said about them on the blogs.**

- **WOMEN: SOME MALE OBSTETRICIANS AND GYNECOLOGISTS (OB/GYN) ARE WAY BETTER THAN SOME FEMALES.**

- Get screened for cancer.

- Read health magazines and blogs to keep up-to-date on the latest health conditions.

- **Occasionally visit the Centers for Disease Control (CDC) website.**

- ❖ Prepare for overseas travel by visiting the Centers for Disease Control (CDC) website.

- ❖ Oral hygiene is very important.

- ❖ Visit your dentist at least once a year to have a checkup and a cleaning.

- ❖ **It's never too late to start paying attention to your health, but it's better to start when you are young.**

- ❖ Celebrity diets are questionable.

- ❖ Celebrities shouldn't be your ideal role model when it comes to dieting or losing weight.

- ❖ It's easier for men to lose weight and build muscle than women.

- ❖ **Learn to cook your own meals to maintain a healthy weight.**

- ❖ Dieting sucks.

- Gastric bypass surgery is the *easy* way of losing weight but you still have to learn to eat healthy.

- Brown bag your lunch occasionally.

- **Starving yourself slows down your metabolism.**

- **Eat five or six small meals throughout the day rather than two large ones.**

- Know your blood type.

- Take a multivitamin daily.

- **Drinking too many energy drinks on a daily basis can be dangerous.**

- Your spou19e should love you regardless of your weight.

- A little pouch is endearing.

- The couple that works out together, stays fit together.

- **Good health is priceless; treasure yours.**

- Too much junk food will kill you.

- **Exercise during your pregnancy, and don't allow yourself to overeat, especially unhealthy foods.**

- Exercising while pregnant can be helpful in maintaining a healthy post pregnancy weight.

- **Don't allow yourself to become a garbage disposal during your pregnancy.**

- Postpartum depression is very real and very serious and should be taken as such.

- **Take your time losing the baby weight, but not fifteen years.**

- ❖ Your weight might negatively affect your ability to get pregnant.

- ❖ Any physical activity is exercise.

- ❖ Take the stairs at least twice a week.

- ❖ **Your mentality plays a huge role in your losing weight.**

- ❖ Invest also in your mental well-being.

- ❖ **Nothing is wrong with seeking professional help for mental issues.**

- ❖ Think of your health in both physical and mental terms.

- ❖ **Take a cardiopulmonary resuscitation (CPR) class.**

- ❖ Promiscuity is unhealthy and grotesque.

- ❖ Pay attention to your sexual health.

- ❖ **It's to your benefit to know your HIV status.**

- ❖ Too much red meat is unhealthy.

- ❖ **Your health should be of the utmost importance to you.**

- ❖ Your body is a temple; treat it as such.

- ❖ Learn to be disciplined when it comes to food.

- ❖ **It's inadvisable to let anyone pressure you into having more food than you want.**

- ❖ Food isn't your enemy—your mind is.

- ❖ Gluttony can kill.

- ❖ Be confident in knowing that you will eventually lose the weight.

- ❖ **Your weight can negatively affect your professional life.**

- Your weight can negatively affect your sex life.

- **NEWSFLASH: MEN STRUGGLE WITH LOSING WEIGHT ALSO.**

- Learn to motivate yourself daily.

- **Under no circumstances should you ever give up on yourself.**

- Having a weight-loss partner can be encouraging.

- **Join a weight-loss program if you need help and motivation.**

- Not everyone is meant to be a size four, and that is OK.

- It's unbeneficial to forgo a healthy weight in favor of fa-fa-fashion.

- **If you don't like what you see in the mirror, you are the only person who can change it.**

- Just because your parents are overweight doesn't mean you have to be also; you are the owner of your destiny. You can always learn healthy eating habits and teach them to your parents.

- **Consistently eating healthily and then having a slice of pizza isn't going to kill you.**

- Research restaurant menus before going out to dinner.

- **Be mindful of your pill-popping habit.**

- As a single man, when was the last time you had a physical?

- **It's unhealthy to sleep with your contacts in; inevitably this might harm your vision.**

- Lasik eye surgery is a good investment.

- Pay close attention also to your dental health.

CHAPTER 6

FINANCES

Introduction

Of the ten topics in this book, the two that I struggle with the most are this one and career.

The movie *2012* (2009) included a scene where people needed to purchase tickets for a Noah's ark–type vessel in order to survive total annihilation. As I watched, I realized that my irresponsibility with money would prevent me from affording tickets for a ship like that one.

My credit card and student loan debt is minimal in comparison to some people, but I still feel like a failure because I have squandered so much money on material items.

When I was growing up, my parents provided me with everything I needed but only a fraction of what I wanted, so as I got older, I felt compelled to get myself everything I wanted regardless of cost or consequences.

Therefore as a young adult and college student, credit card companies targeted me and shoved credit card applications in my face, and I thought, hey, now I can afford all those things I wanted when I was younger.

Here's what credit card companies don't tell young adults and college students: they still have to pay that money back with interest. Credit cards are not free money.

I believe that if you charge it you should pay for it or at least make an effort to join a debt consolidation program to repay what you owe.

Once in my early college years, I was flat broke and probably had thirty-five dollars in my checking account. I sat on the floor in my room surrounded by all the crap I had accumulated and thought to myself this is a contemporary form of misery.

You really need to take time to examine why you feel you need all this stuff. Who are you trying to impress by letting people think you are something you are not? Friend, I've been there and done that and have the receipts to prove it.

You shouldn't base your value on the things you accumulate over time; they are inanimate objects, which in the long run are worthless.

Recently, I was watching a documentary called *Client 9: The Rise and Fall of Eliot Spitzer*, and a billionaire in it commented that he had been both poor and rich and being rich is better. I agree to some extent; it's good to be financially stable, but it also matters how you make your money.

Life is about lessons and as I've gotten older I have become wiser, and for all the money in the world, you couldn't get me to sign up for a credit card.

My dad used to tell me and siblings when we were younger that, "A fool and his money are soon parted," and he was right. I'm living proof of that.

* * *

- ❖ **A person should make the money; money shouldn't make the person.**

- ❖ Use your money to buy things instead of people.

- ❖ Be wise and financially invest in your future.

- ❖ Learn to be a good manager of your money.

- ❖ **If you don't trust yourself with other people's money, stay away from it.**

- ❖ Be just as cautious with other people's money as you are with yours.

- ❖ It's reckless to steal your clients' money to pay for your partner's expensive taste.

- ❖ **Integrity is priceless.**

- ❖ Money can get you a pretty girlfriend, but it will never make her love you.

- Being rich can make you paranoid.

- **If your friend is having financial difficulties, it's better to give than to lend him or her money with the agreement that this is a one-time occurrence.**

- Only lend money to someone who you know will not be back for more.

- **Never cosign for the debt of an irresponsible person.**

- Credit card companies want to bankrupt your future; it's reckless to let them!

- **Credit card debt is a contemporary form of slavery.**

- Research credit cards thoroughly before applying for one.

- **VISIT: WWW.CREDITCARDS.COM**

- **Be urgent about paying off your credit card debt.**

  - Always pay off credit cards with higher interest rates first.

  - It's better to have student loan than credit card debt.

- **DOCUMENTARY: <u>MAXED OUT: HARD TIMES, EASY CREDIT, AND THE ERA OF PREDATORY LENDERS</u> (2006)**

  - Better to save now and spend later than to spend now and worry about paying off later.

- **It's never wise to spend based on future earnings; wait until you have money in the bank before spending it.**

  - Borrowing against your future income to pay for your present expenses is irresponsible.

  - There's nothing wrong with having a closet full of shoes as long as you are not using your rent money to pay for them.

❖ Money ≠ Class

- ❖ Money can't buy you good character, but it sure can buy you fancy things, which mean nothing if your character is funky.

❖ You don't need money to live a rich life.

- ❖ Make sure you have at least three months' living expenses saved up.

- ❖ Under no circumstances should you give your credit or debit card information to someone you just met on the street who is supposedly soliciting for a nonprofit organization.

- ❖ Money doesn't grow on trees, nor is it free.

❖ Free money is trouble and can get you into precarious situations.

- ❖ Your desire for an extravagant lifestyle can put you in precarious situations.

- ❖ If your motto is more money, more money, more money, no amount of money will satisfy you.

- It's never too late to learn the value of a dollar.

- **No money in the world can buy you into heaven.**

- Sometimes leasing a car is a better option than buying one.

- Be wary of cosigning for other people's debt.

- You shouldn't invest more than one-fourth of your net worth.

- **Only invest what you are willing to lose and can live without.**

- It's reckless to use one debt to pay off another.

- Watch the person watching your money.

- **Enjoy your money because when you die you might leave it to someone who is going to be reckless with it.**

- ❖ If you are married, you should both know what is going on with the household finances; no one person should be responsible.

- ❖ To keep yourself aloof of the financial situation in your marriage is foolish.

❖ READ: "THE ROAD TO WEALTH" BY SUZE ORMAN

- ❖ It's not recommended to just read a Suze Orman book; instead, absorb and apply its principles.

- ❖ There's nothing wrong with a woman making more money than her spouse.

- ❖ As an adult, you should know how to manage your money, and if you do not, find someone to teach you.

❖ A fool and his money will undoubtedly be separated.

- ❖ Keeping up with the Joneses is going to leave you flat broke.

- ❖ It's foolish to exaggerate about your financial situation to impress anyone.

- **If you can't afford it, *you just can't afford it.***

  - Be satisfied with what you can afford and stop lusting after what you can't.

- **Don't be one of those people who spend so much time lusting for the possessions of others that you never take time to enjoy your abundant life.**

  - Stop obsessing over other people's money, and go make your own.

- **Living within your means is wise.**

  - Learn to be financially independent.

- **Let no one control your money.**

  - Give no one access to your bank account(s).

- ❖ It's unwise to let anyone make you feel guilty for being financially savvy.

- ❖ **Save for a rainy day because one day it will pour.**

- ❖ Plan your spending, and don't buy on impulse.

- ❖ Always pay with cash or a debit card.

- ❖ It's unwise to use credit cards for small purchases.

- ❖ **Always pay off your credit card balance monthly if you can afford to.**

- ❖ It's reckless to take out cash advances from your credit cards.

- ❖ Always pay attention to the fine print on credit card brochures.

- ❖ **It's imprudent to cash out or borrow from your 401(k) to pay off your credit card debt.**

- ❖ Put yourself in a position to lend and not to borrow.

- ❖ Only borrow money from people you trust and not people who will throw it in your face later.

- ❖ **Money can ruin a friendship.**

- ❖ Money can't sustain a friendship that has already disintegrated.

- ❖ **Check your credit report and score at least twice a year.**

- ❖ Always work to improve your credit score.

- ❖ Always open your mail.

- ❖ **Keep your social security number confidential.**

- ❖ It's foolish to open a department store account for a measly 15 percent discount.

- ❖ **Document all business transactions.**

- If you are an entrepreneur, know what is going on with your accounting books.

- Always pay your taxes and on time, or Uncle Sam will get you...eventually.

- **It took time to get into credit card debt; it will also take time to get out, so be patient.**

- Learn from your mistakes and pass along those lessons.

- Know your partner's credit score before getting married.

- If you marry a financially irresponsible person who loves to shop and you get divorced. his or her debt collectors will pursue you to recoup their money.

- **Make sure your spouse is responsible for his or her debt.**

- Work on lowering your debt instead of trying to find a rich person to pay it off.

- Try to pay off the majority of your debt before getting married, so you don't bring any financial baggage into the marriage.

- ❖ **Instead of incurring more debt by buying things you don't need, stop spending and work to decrease it.**

- ❖ Join a debt consolidation program if your debt is getting out of control.

- ❖ **Being on a debt consolidation payment plan can be one of the smartest financial decisions you ever make.**

- ❖ Bankruptcy shouldn't be your first choice when trying to become debt-free.

- ❖ **If you can't realistically afford and elaborate wedding ceremony, consider investing in a destination wedding package. This can be**

very cost-effective depending on location.

❖ It doesn't make sense to borrow money to pay for a lavish wedding where attendees feast on Beluga caviar only to return from your honeymoon to a basement apartment.

❖ When your child is born, set up college funds for him or her immediately.

❖ If you don't have a 401(k) or a retirement plan, you can't afford to pay for your children's college.

❖ Let your children know about the family's financial situation before it's too late.

❖ No money in the world can buy you good children.

❖ Divorce is especially unpleasant if you are stuck with your ex-spouse's debt.

❖ It's necessary to have a life insurance policy, especially if people are depending on you financially.

- **Be careful to whom you hand over power of attorney.**

  - Give sacrificially to the church, but not under duress.

- **Money given to the church shouldn't be used to pay off children sexually abused by priests.**

  - It's inadvisable to borrow money from coworkers; it will blow up in your face if things turn sour.

- **Not everyone lives on credit cards; strive to be one of the people who doesn't.**

  - One of the benefits of working hard is that one day you will get to enjoy the fruits of your labor; to prematurely start enjoying it before it has materialized is foolish and will cost you more in the long run.

- **Most credit card companies prey on the young and dumb.**

- His money is his money; your money is your money.

- **Know the difference between credit cards and charge cards.**

- Credit cards should be used for necessities, not wants.

- **If you allow someone to use your credit card or debit card, you are responsible for his or her charges.**

- Have at least one checking account and one savings account.

- **As soon as you get a job that offers a 401(k), invest in it.**

- You are never too old to start investing in a 401(k) plan.

FINANCES

- Keep on top of deposits to your 401(k). Build a nice cushy retirement plan for yourself.

- **Start financially planning for your old age as soon as possible.**

- Build a nice cushy retirement plan for yourself.

- **Work to make money and make that money work for you.**

- Save at least 25 percent of every paycheck.

- Think in terms of wealth, not riches.

- **Money earned by ill-gotten means only haunts the owners.**

- Learn to create a budget and stick to it.

- Having children isn't cheap.

- **If you are struggling financially, having a tribe of children will**

make you even more financially strapped.

❖ If your parents are wealthy, don't let anyone make you feel guilty about that fact.

❖ What you do with money is the root of all evil.

❖ **Living from paycheck to paycheck is irresponsible.**

❖ Some people live paycheck to paycheck but are some of the happiest and richest human beings alive.

❖ It's imprudent to take out a second mortgage on your home to pay for your child's wedding.

❖ **It's financially irresponsible to take out a second mortgage to pay for your child's wedding, but if you do and he or she is divorced in two years, make sure he or she pays you back every penny.**

- Bragging about being rich will get you robbed.

- **Posting pictures of yourself on social media surrounded by wads of cash—in this depressed economy—is an invitation to robbers.**

- Be careful whom you invite over to your palatial estate.

- **Be generous but not foolish with your finances.**

- It's risky to donate money unless you know exactly what it's being used for.

- **If you are wealthy, develop social and economic programs to help the less fortunate.**

- Your money shouldn't be your god.

- The more you give, the more you get.

- ❖ **Every little bit adds up.**

- ❖ You are not entitled to a rich person's money.

- ❖ **You can't blame affluent people for taking advantage of various tax breaks because if you were in the same position, wouldn't you do the same?**

- ❖ Just because you are a financially savvy Christian doesn't mean you are supposed to use your money to consistently bail out other financially irresponsible Christians.

- ❖ **God financially blesses the rich, and he's willing to do the same for you.**

- ❖ Not everyone is as rich as he or she pretends to be.

- ❖ **It's imprudent to become consumed with making money.**

- Use your money to build up and not to tear down. However, there will be times when you will have to tear down to rebuild bigger and better.

- Whether you have thousands or millions of dollars, prenuptial agreements are necessary.

- **Be generous to your children, but it's unwise to use your money to compensate for not being there.**

- If it's your time to die, no amount of money can give you an extra second.

- **It's inadvisable to take out a loan in order to pay for a fancy funeral; instead, have the person cremated.**

- A fiscally irresponsible chief executive officer is detrimental to any organization.

❖ MUSIC: "AIN'T NOTHIN' GOIN' ON BUT THE RENT" BY GWEN GUTHRIE

- ❖ There's nothing wrong with wanting to be rich, but why do you *really* want to be rich?

- ❖ To ensure a financially secure future, don't be one of those fools who carelessly squanders money to purchase items he or she can't afford to impress people he or she doesn't like.

- ❖ **There's no money like the money you worked hard for.**

- ❖ If you have good health, count your blessings because some rich people envy you tremendously.

- ❖ **At some point in your life, you are going to realize that you can't afford to be broke.**

- ❖ Being broke isn't beneficial to you, but is advantageous to your creditors.

CHAPTER 7

RELATIONSHIPS

* * *

Introduction

This section is primarily about romantic relationships, a topic with which I don't have much experience; thus, most of these anecdotes are from my family, friends, coworkers, and situations that I've been privy to.

I consider myself an old school lover because I love hand-written letters, I like when a man opens my car door, and I think it's wonderful when a man calls simply to ask how I am doing. Apparently, a whole lot has changed since Sam Cooke crooned, "I Love You for Sentimental Reasons."

From what I've observed, romantic relationships have evolved over the last few decades quite rapidly and not necessarily for the best. For instance, some women/wives are comfortable with their men/husbands calling them bitches, and men are comfortable with their high-profile wives being absent from home for weeks at a time.

By no means am I trying to tell anyone how behave in his or her relationship because I believe most couples know what works for them; however, I'm concerned about the example that's being set for our young people. Some adults don't realize the message they are sending to the young people in their lives when they choose to participate in some of these relationships. Most children or young people emulate the behavior of the adults in their lives whether the adult is aware of it or not.

I believe in being fruitful and multiplying but I also believe that boyfriends and husbands shouldn't be getting the same benefits. Women should not be acting as wives unless there is a marriage certificate with her and her partner's name on it, and men should not be paying rent for a woman's apartment unless she's his wife or unfortunately his children's mother.

In order for most relationships to be successful and thrive, I think it helps a great deal if each individual getting into the relationship has a clear understanding of who he or she is as a person and his or her needs in a relationship.

***
In General

- ### **The most important part of any relationship is the beginning.**

- A spontaneous interaction can be the beginning of a wonderful relationship.

- A wonderful relationship can originate from the unlikeliest of circumstances.

- ### **Some relationships are for a season while others will last a lifetime.**

- The healthiest relationships have boundaries.

- ### **To keep the peace in your relationship, you will *have* to learn to agree to disagree.**

- To make your relationship work, you will have to be *sacrificial* and at times *silent*.

- ❖ **Develop a deep friendship first before you get into a sexual relationship.**

  - ❖ Set your relationship up to win by getting to know the person before jumping into the sack.

  - ❖ Build your relationship on a solid foundation (friendship) rather than on orgasms.

- ❖ **One of the reasons most relationships don't work out is because people have sex first and then try to get to know each other after.**

  - ❖ Without sex, what kind of relationship do you really have?

- ❖ **Sex clouds sensible judgment.**

  - ❖ Sex makes usually smart people stupid.

  - ❖ Just because you are sleeping with someone doesn't mean you are in a monogamous relationship.

- ❖ **Sex ≠ Intimacy**

- ❖ There's so much more to intimacy than sex.

- ❖ **Far too many people underestimate the potency of lust.**

- ❖ Unless there's a marriage certificate, you are single.

- ❖ **Your relationship status can only be one of the following: single, married, separated, or divorced.**

- ❖ Celebrate your single life.

- ❖ **Find peace and contentment in your single status.**

- ❖ It's not recommended to use the phrase "I love you" carelessly.

- ❖ **Do you know what it means to genuinely love**

someone? Find out before making that declaration.

- Learn to love yourself first before getting into a relationship.

- Love means never saying, "I quit."

- **Love should mean having to say, "I'm sorry" over and over again, and genuinely meaning it.**

- Love can make a marriage work if you both understand what the real meaning of love is from 1 Corinthians 13:4–7.

- **Some people want to get married, but are unwilling to put in the time and energy needed to make the marriage work.**

- Marriage is primarily about love, respect, trust, communication, forgiveness, and sacrifice.

- **It's not about what you say, but what the person you said it to thought they heard.**

- It's unwise to let yourself settle for a marriage based on peaceful indifference.

- **Be careful what you say to each other during arguments.**

- It's unproductive to use your partner's past against him or her.

- **Hurt + Hurt = More Hurt**

- **Only a fool bites the hand that feeds him or her.**

- Just because you survived a near-death experience doesn't mean you should marry your rescuer.

- ❖ **Most people don't know what good love is until they experience it.**

- ❖ In order to be a good spouse/partner, you have to be willing to fi7ht for and with the person you are in a relationship with.

- ❖ **Before you marry someone, by all means have those freaky and uncomfortable conversations.**

- ❖ If you are a freak, marry another freak even if you are a Christian.

- ❖ Be honest with the person you are in relationship with; this is to say, if you don't feel comfortable with his or her freakiness, let it be known.

- ❖ **It's deceitful to pretend to like your partner's friends only to scorn them when you get married.**

RELATIONSHIPS

- The trickery you bring into your relationship will eventually catch up to you.

- Your partner isn't a mind reader; learn to verbalize your exact feelings.

- **To know your needs in a relationship, you have to get to know yourself.**

- A married person can't be your boyfriend or girlfriend.

- **READ: "THE FIVE LOVE LANGUAGES" BY DR. GARY CHAPMAN**

- Just because you don't love yourself doesn't mean no one else will.

- **Sometimes outsiders will have to teach you how to love yourself.**

- Relationships are complicated, especially when you are always right.

- Be careful whom you let your spirit entwine with.

- Not all relationships should be intimate or sexual ones.

- **Healthy relationships flow in harmony.**

- Friends tell you what you need to hear, and enemies tell you what you want to hear.

- Make sure you and your partner are on the same page about where your relationship is heading.

- **Keep the number of outsiders in your relationship to a minimum.**

- What happens in your relationship should be primarily between you and your partner; it shouldn't be for public consumption.

- Having too many outsiders in your relationship can complicate it.

- **To get to know the person you are in a relationship with, you will need to study him or her.**

- ❖ Be careful whom you get input from on your relationship.

- ❖ Allow and encourage your significant other to be him- or herself in order to feel comfortable around you.

- ❖ An illusion of a perfect relationship isn't fooling anyone but you.

- ❖ **Learn to be self-controlled and disciplined when it comes to matters of the heart.**

- ❖ Lust has more to do with the mind than the body.

- ❖ **If you are not an active participant in your relationship, you are in the wrong relationship.**

- ❖ It's good to go on dates because dating helps you to discover your needs in a relationship.

- ❖ **It's OK to date and marry outside your race depending on which continent you live on.**

- Be an equal-opportunity dater.

- **It's best to date people who are spiritually professionally, and psychologically your equal; you cheat yourself when you do otherwise.**

- Without trust, your relationship is doomed.

- **It can take a lifetime to get to know someone.**

- It's ill-advised to give too much too soon; take it nice and slow.

- **Your sweetness shouldn't be considered the neighborhood or office sampler, where everyone gets a taste.**

- Love shouldn't hurt unless you are both masochists.

- Masochism might be fun, but be careful because some people don't know where to draw the line.

❖ Lust ≠ Love

- Lust and love are not friends; they are opposites.

❖ It's good to know the difference between love and lust music.

- If the only time you get along is in the bedroom, your relationship is destined to fail.

- It takes more than sex to maintain a healthy relationship.

- A healthy relationship isn't built on sex.

❖ Dating a married person probably isn't going to turn out well for you.

- If you don't respect other people's relationships, no one will respect yours.

- It's reckless to talk trash about your spouse to strangers.

- Stick to one relationship at a time.

- ❖ **If you can't be with the one you love, respect the one you are with.**

- ❖ You have to respect each other both in and out of the bedroom.

- ❖ **No one, including you, changes overnight, so stop expecting and dem1nding it.**

- ❖ It's not your job to change your spouse/partner.

- ❖ Take the person as is or leave him or her alone.

- ❖ **If you don't want to have babies out of wedlock, then practice abstinence or safe sex.**

- ❖ There's definitely a thin line between love and hate.

- ❖ Your best friend today could be your worst enemy tomorrow.

- ❖ **Jealous spouses might initially be endearing;**

however, after a while, they become a nightmare.

- As thrilling as it might seem, it's ill-advised to mix business with pleasure.

❖ Mixing business with pleasure can lead to a messy situation.

- A relationship is an investment, and you shouldn't invest more than you are willing to lose.

- It's ill-advised to give everything to a relationship unless you are willing to lose it all.

❖ Don't assume you are going to get married; make sure.

❖ Never be afraid to walk away from an unhealthy relationship.

- Effective communication is an art; learn it.

- ❖ **Be quick to listen and slow to speak.**

  - ❖ Honesty is always the best policy in relationships.

  - ❖ If you are afraid to be honest with the person you are in a relationship with, that is a major problem.

- ❖ **There should be no intermingling of funds unless you are married.**

  - ❖ Learn to entertain yourself without masturbating.

- ❖ **Healthy relationships don't happen overnight; they develop over time.**

  - ❖ Value and appreciate the person you are in a relationship with.

  - ❖ A nagging spouse is just plain nagging.

- ❖ **The ex-lovers of friends should be off-limits.**

  - ❖ It's reckless to date friends of your siblings.

- Just because you are married doesn't mean you should dump your single friends.

- **In your relationship you should regularly be discovering something new and wonderful about yourself and your partner.**

- Your relationship should be thriving and getting better with time.

- Your relationship should refine you into a better person. If it's not, you are in the wrong relationship.

- **It's reckless to ignore signs of danger ahead in your relationship.**

- Always trust your instincts when it comes to your relationship.

- **Look before you leap into a potentially bad marriage.**

- If it seems too good to be true, it usually is.

- Sometimes not trusting in a relationship has more to do with you and less with your significant other.

- **It's unfair to demand complete trust of your partner and then be unwilling to trust him or her.**

- Your manipulative ways will only last for a season.

- Tricks can't stop your partner from walking out the door.

- **A person is irreplaceable, but the foolishness they bring into a relationship is very much replaceable.**

- **Every couple knows what works best for them in their relationship; learn to respect their decisions.**

- Your parents' relationship has a huge influence on the way you view relationships.

- Just because your parents had an unhealthy relationship doesn't mean you can't have a healthy one.

- **Learn from the relationship failures of your parents.**

- Associate with couples that are in healthy relationships.

- When was the last time you were single?

- **Jumping from relationship to relationship is unhealthy.**

- The truth is in the eyes.

- If you struggle with lust, stay away from lustful material.

- **Anyone can find a bedroom buddy, but not everyone knows how to choose the right life partner.**

❖ There's nothing wrong if you are waiting until you get married to have sex.

- ❖ There's nothing wrong with being a virgin in your thirties.

- ❖ Be completely honest about your sexual situation before getting married.

❖ It's not right to trick someone into marriage.

- ❖ It's unbeneficial to use someone's love for you against him or her.

- ❖ If you don't want or like children, let your future spouse know before getting married.

❖ If you can't have children, let your future spouse know as soon as possible.

- ❖ If you have children living in another country, your future spouse should know this before signing the marriage certificate.

- ❖ **If you have children, your future spouse should know that it's a package deal and be genuinely happy with that.**

- ❖ A couple should have major discussions about finances, babies, where to live, and so on before getting married.

- ❖ Enjoy a couple of years of marriage before complicating your situation with children.

- ❖ **Running a background check on your future spouse behind his or her back is deceitful.**

- ❖ If you don't trust the person you are in a relationship with, then you should get out of the relationship.

- ❖ Marriages come and go, but your ex-spouse's debt—that you acquired during your marriage—will last long after he or she is gone.

- ❖ **MOVIE: <u>HE'S JUST NOT THAT INTO YOU</u>**

❖ Know what triggers your anger and how to defuse it.

❖ **Just because you love someone a certain way doesn't mean he or she will return love in the same way.**

❖ Don't waste your time in a relationship in which you are being treated badly.

❖ **Sometimes you have to cut your losses and move on from a bad romance.**

❖ To truly move on from a bad romance, you have to sever the ties that bind.

❖ Know what a healthy relationship looks like.

❖ Seek outside help if there's physical and emotional abuse.

❖ **If you are a Christian in an unhealthy marriage with another Christian, sometimes it's wise to**

seek professional help outside the church.

- If you consistently attract the same unhealthy people, look inside.

- **If you constantly have to convince yourself that you should be in your relationship, it's time to bid it adieu.**

- Always look for ways to improve yourself within your relationship.

- It might be a good idea to go to marriage counseling before you tie the knot.

- **Marriage is a delightful experience, but not everyone will succeed at it.**

- Marriage is the ultimate commitment.

- Marriage should be like a treasure hunt: you are always discovering something new and delightful about your spouse.

- ❖ **Care more about making your marriage last than about planning for the wedding ceremony.**

- ❖ Marry someone who inspires you to be your best, or he or she will suck the life out of you.

- ❖ **There's nothing wrong with only wanting to swap DNA with your future spouse.**

- ❖ Regardless of the advice offered, you are going to do what and who you want.

- ❖ Present future mates to your parents respectfully.

- ❖ You can't tame a person's heart.

- ❖ When the one you love is in love with someone else, you have to give him or her room to figure things out for him or herself.

- ❖ **To perpetually live in fear that your spouse is**

going to leave you can be debilitating.

❖ Love is a fight and both partners have to be willing to get into the ring to duke it out (not an inference to domestic violence).

❖ Some people cheat and some people are simply cheaters.

❖ **It's easy to forgive someone who is being demonized because of your reckless actions.**

❖ You have to love yourself and your significant other enough to let him or her go if he or she no longer wants to be in a relationship with you.

❖ The only thing that trumps marrying for money is marrying for character.

❖ **Women:** If want forgiveness from a husband who loves you because you maxed out his card or did something stupid, start with: <u>I Apologize</u> by Anita Baker > <u>All the Man I Need</u> by Whitney Houston > <u>Let's Get it On</u> by Marvin Gaye > **Wait 30 mins** > <u>Let's Do it Again</u> by Staples Singers > <u>From this Moment On</u> by Shania Twain.

***
Women

- **To love thyself is to respect thyself.**

- Sex ≠ Love

- Lust will get you pregnant on the first date.

- **Lust will get you four children and no husband.**

- Once the feeling of lust is awakened in a man's heart it's very difficult for that feeling to once again become dormant.

- **If you subscribe to a ninety-day rule or five-date rule before sleeping with a man, don't tell him as this will awakens the hunter in him.**

- Most men can be very patient when they want to be.

- It's ill-advised to be a calculating woman; instead be a calculus woman.

- **If you are giving it up without any form of commitment required, there will be men lining up to take it without any form of commitment.**

- If you have been having sex for the last eighteen years and have never received flowers at work from one of your lovers, you are sleeping with the wrong men.

- **If you have been having sex since you were twelve-years-old and are currently in your thirties with no husband, it's time to give your body a rest.**

- Most men love and need to feel loved and needed.

- Love, need, and want your husband or someone else will.

- ❖ **Most men place value on women, so if you act cheap, they will treat you as such.**

- ❖ Some men simply don't know how to value a good woman.

- ❖ **If you want to be taken seriously, conduct yourself respectfully.**

- ❖ **No man wants to marry the town's sperm depository.**

- ❖ A decent man isn't going to abandon you because of your standards.

- ❖ The man who is best for you respects your decisions.

- ❖ Have deep-rooted convictions and stick to them.

- ❖ **A man will test you based on your convictions.**

- ❖ It's not advantageous to be easily swayed.

- ❖ **If you are saving it for marriage, don't give it up for carats.**

- ❖ **Men choose wives, but you choose the father of your children.**

- ❖ The mo19t important decision of your life is choosing the right man to be the father of your children.

- ❖ Are you sure you want that dude to be the father of your child?

- ❖ **Make it easy on yourself by only sleeping with men who share the same core values as you do.**

- ❖ Somewhere along the way, some women have let some men brainwash them into thinking that, in order for a relationship to work, sex before marriage is necessary. That is simply not true.

- ❖ A man understands the truth, so if he asks you a question, tell him the truth.

- ❖ **If you don't want to know if you look fat in that dress, don't ask.**

- ❖ In most relationships, men tend to gravitate toward the leadership role because they like teaching, so don't worry about it and let them teach you something occasionally.

- ❖ **Just because you are self-sufficient doesn't mean you don't need a man for *some* things.**

- ❖ You are probably out of his league; hence, he doesn't know how to treat you.

- ❖ **The main reason you are a victim in your relationship is because you choose to be.**

- ❖ There is an illuminating and prosperous life after an abusive relationship.

- ❖ **You don't have to get pregnant if you don't want to.**

- There's a difference between high maintenance and gold digging.

- **Shacking up arrangements will *always* work out better for him than you.**

- Shacking up with a man prepares him to be a husband, but not necessarily yours.

- If you have been shacking up with a man for over ten years and have a child with him, why should he marry you?

- It doesn't make sense to pay him to *do* you.

- **If you have to ask a man what you mean to him, you probably don't mean much to him.**

- He's supposed to ask you to move in, and you are supposed to say no.

- Surround yourself with people who have healthy concepts of relationships.

- ❖ **Your bitter girlfriends might be the ones keeping you from healthy relationships; hence, they need to go ASAP.**

- ❖ Take all the time necessary to get to know yourself, realizing that it might take a lifetime.

- ❖ **Not all men are gods or dogs.**

- ❖ It's foolish to depend on a man to define you.

- ❖ **You have to break the cycle of sleeping with every man that crosses your path who drives a Maserati. How do you know that's its actually his and not borrowed or rented.**

- ❖ Some men already know that by unlocking their Lamborghini, some women will unlock their legs. Don't be one of those women.

- **Not every man deserves a taste of your sweetness.**

- Treat yourself to a day of pampering occasionally.

- **Treat yourself to a Brazilian wax at least once in your life.**

- If a man tells you, "You look better with the lights off," you might want to reevaluate your relationship.

- **Sleeping with a large number of men diminishes your value.**

- If you don't know who you are, read the Bible.

- Love is primarily about actions and not words.

- **Pay more attention to a man's actions than his words.**

- A responsible and actionable man is a breath of fresh air.

- **The best man is the man whose actions match his words.**

- If he can't make it across the room to say hi, he's just not that into you.

- **Just because you make more money than your boyfriend doesn't mean you should always throw it in his face.**

- No matter how much money you make, never pay his rent.

- **Your money gives you power and provides you with options.**

- His money isn't your money, so stop depending on it and get your own.

- **Dating or marrying a rich person doesn't make you rich.**

- Let no one get his or her claws on your money.

- You are paying his rent not because he needs you to, but because you want to.

- **Yes is yes and no is found in his excuses.**

- If you are depressed, a baby isn't going to solve the problem.

- **One of the reasons some men lie to you so much is because you are extremely gullible and don't ask follow-up questions.**

- A man can spot an insecure woman from a mile away.

- Some men will attempt to raise their mothers from the grave to get into your pants and then pull a Harry Houdini.

- **Some men are willing to abide by your rules until they get what they want and then they are out of there.**

- If he dumps you, beds you, dumps you, you are not the one—you are just old reliable.

- **A man usually asks a woman to marry him when he's ready to be the man she needs him to be.**

- When a man wants to get married, he's going to get married.

- **It doesn't take a man five years to marry the woman he loves.**

- When a man finds a woman he loves, he's willing to risk getting married to her even though she has six children by four different men and his entire family—including his dog—hates her.

- **When a man finds a woman he loves, he marries her quickly because he doesn't want another man to discover what he has found in her.**

- If he waits years and years to marry you, you are probably not his first choice.

- **Under no circumstances should you ever propose to your boyfriend.**

- It's never wise to underestimate a man.

- If you think men don't know what they want, you are not that sharp.

- **It's risky to ingratiate yourself to men; they know exactly who and what they want.**

- If he doesn't claim you publicly, you are probably just a hit and run.

- **The game is set up to give men the upper hand, but if he loves you, he's willing to share, compromise, or even let you run the show.**

- ❖ No matter how hard you try, you can't make a man love you.

- ❖ Why doesn't he love you? He probably doesn't know; all he knows is that you are not the one he wants to spend a lifetime with.

- ❖ **Teach and show him how to love you.**

- ❖ Taps on the shoulder at 2:00 a.m. can get you pregnant.

- ❖ When a man is in love with you, you always know where he is, and you *never* have to monitor him.

- ❖ **It's unproductive and depressing to waste your time with mama's boys.**

- ❖ Be more interested in his character than his pocketbook.

- ❖ **If you can't find a man, import one…maybe.**

- ❖ Time isn't going to be kind or forgiving to you, so don't waste it.

- It's unproductive to waste your time with the wrong guy because that only delays the right one.

- **It's unbeneficial to waste your youth chasing after rich men—they will only use and discard you.**

- Don't waste your time with a man who has a whole bunch of children with a whole bunch of women; he can't do much for you, and his paycheck is already accounted for.

- Know what you want out of a relationship.

- **It's careless to give up your dreams to let your boyfriend achieve his.**

- Have your own life and group of friends.

- It's unwise to let your significant other pressure you into giving up your friends.

- Good friendships are hard to come by, so don't take yours for granted.

- **One of the reasons your significant other wants you to give up your friends is because he doesn't want anyone to shed light on the rubbish he's feeding you.**

- Some men like to keep you isolated because they want to be the only ones to influence your decisions.

- **It's unfortunate that you are fearless when it comes to fighting your boyfriend's battles but fearful of fighting your own.**

- It's regrettable that you allow your spouse to define you and can't imagine your life without him.

- Stay away from men with several children by several women (there are very few situations where this is acceptable).

- **Prince Harry is still single, but you can't**

show up at Buckingham Palace with illegitimate children trailing behind you.

❖ A man of fine character is divine.

❖ He doesn't have to be a millionaire to be your shining star.

❖ **A man's love is priceless.**

❖ Get your priorities straight when looking for a mate.

❖ Think in terms of life partner instead of a bedroom buddy.

❖ **You are already complete; now let yourself be found by someone who compliments you.**

❖ It's reckless to jump out of the frying pan into the fire; that is to say, don't leave one bad situation only to get into an even worse one.

❖ What is a lovely young lady like you doing with a guy like him?

- **There's more to a man than the size of his schlong.**

- Your children should be the love of your life.

- It's unbeneficial to allow yourself to be trapped in a horrible relationship because of good sex.

- **Sheer laziness on your part is what keeps you in a horrible relationship with that rich, disrespectful, misogynistic douche bag.**

- A prenuptial agreement might be a good idea.

- **It could be financially detrimental to sign a prenuptial agreement under duress.**

- Your prenuptial agreement should include a clause about cheating.

- **When it comes to signing a prenuptial agreement, his lawyers are working in his best interest; therefore, get your own lawyers.**

- The true character of your future spouse is revealed if he asks you to sign a prenuptial agreement two d1ys before your wedding.

- **A prenuptial agreement is a business arrangement; make sure you are satisfied with *all* the terms before you sign.**

- You don't have to be a millionaire to have a will.

- Contemporary men are looking to marry women who have their own money.

- **Just because he proposed in front of your family doesn't**

mean you should say yes.

- Some men will try to manipulate you into marriage; be on your guard.

- A man will enlist the help of your desperate Aunt Betty to con you into marrying him.

- Just because he asks you to marry him doesn't mean you should say yes.

❖ It's better to be single than in a relationship with a married man.

- If he's cheating on his wife with you, what do you think he will do if he leaves her for you?

- If your nana is so ill, why has he not left his wife?

❖ Just because he cheated on you doesn't mean you should do the same to him.

- Complete your education even if you are dating a rich person.

- Diversify your relationships.

- **Pursue your dreams instead of men.**

- If a man has a girlfriend, let him be.

- **If he *loves* and *wants* to be with you so much, why is he still with her?**

- Why are you upset or bitter because your ex–live-in boyfriend of six years dumped you six months ago and is now married with a baby on the way?

- It's unproductive to pick a fight with your ex-boyfriend's new girlfriend; she doesn't have anything to do with your breakup.

- **If your ex-boyfriend dumped you and married another woman, why are you still sleeping with him?**

- If he doesn't want to marry and have a baby with you, that says a lot.

- ❖ **Some men don't want to dump you but certainly will never marry you.**

- ❖ Most men have no concept or appreciation for time—it's not part of their DNA.

- ❖ **You have to teach men to respect your time.**

- ❖ Using your money to try to control a man is useless.

- ❖ **Marriage before babies because you don't want to be stuck with some dude's illegitimate child.**

- ❖ Being childless keeps you free and available to date whomever you choose.

- ❖ Most men prefer to marry childless women even though they might have some children of their own.

- ❖ **Some men knock you up to tie you down.**

❖ **Very few men genuinely want to be with a woman with four children.**

❖ Men know what other men find unattractive in women, and they use it to their advantage. Don't let a man make you unattractive.

❖ Don't fall for this line: I'm ready to be a father but not a husband.

❖ **If you think it's better to be in a relationship with a woman than a man, you are kidding yourself. It's not about gender; it's about character.**

❖ A househusband can end up costing you a pretty penny in the end.

❖ It's risky to hire a sixteen-year-old with perky boobs to babysit your children if your husband is sexually frustrated.

❖ **You can't stop your significant other from cheating; if he wants to**

cheat, he's going to cheat.

❖ There's no surefire way to prevent your boyfriend from cheating on you.

❖ **Cheating in a marriage is forgivable, depending on the situation.**

❖ If you are going to forgive your husband for cheating, you shouldn't keep throwing it in his face every chance you get.

❖ **Before you embark on the arduous task of dumping your cheating husband, get advice.**

❖ Make sure you are dumping your cheating husband because you want to and not because you are being pressured to.

❖ **If you want to get rid of a man permanently, let him dump you.**

❖ If your boyfriend cheats on you, dump him expeditiously.

- If he dumps you and then wants to get back together, have a list of requirements.

- Men don't marry women they can't trust.

- **Even though "I love you" floats off some men's lips with ease, very few actually mean it.**

- Some men know that saying, "I love you" unlocks some women's legs; don't be one of those women.

- Saying, "I love you," should be confirmation of what is already felt in your relationship.

- **If your boyfriend loves you, you should feel it before he actually says it.**

- A kiss on the forehead might be endearing but don't let it get you knocked up on the first date.

- You are way too hot to be begging him to stay.

- ❖ **Be strategic in both business and relationships.**

  - ❖ Approach your relationships strategically. Most men do what is in their best interest; therefore, you should do the same.

- ❖ **Forget trying to get 17 percent of a man's paycheck by deliberately getting pregnant; instead, go for his heart.**

  - ❖ Some women intentionally get pregnant by a rich man, so they can collect child support, but the joke is on these women because some men don't mind paying child support because they know they will never be there for her or their child. Don't be one of these women.

  - ❖ A man supposedly needs a reason to marry, and if he has had you every which way, he will probably marry someone else.

- ❖ **Men like novelty, so you had better learn to be**

adventurous in your marriage.

❖ **Your hips don't lie, so know how to move them.**

❖ If you have been dating a man for over 2½ years and there's no discussion of marriage, you might want to look elsewhere.

❖ **Some men don't want to marry you, but they also don't want another man to have you.**

❖ Some men will try to tie you down with promises; let them know you need more than promises.

❖ Some men are just sexually using you until they find the woman they want to marry.

❖ **Every man wants to be married or remarried including George Clooney, and as soon as he meets the woman he**

needs, he will marry her.

- Every man wants to get married; he just doesn't want to marry you although he will use you as long as you let him.

- You should never have to prove to a man why you are marriage material.

- **Learn to make a good sandwich because some men really appreciate this *rare* talent.**

- If you think sex is all you have to offer in a relationship, you are sadly mistaken.

- There's something called the illusion of happiness.

- **It's reckless to be a tease; if you don't want to have sex with a man, don't bring him back to your apartment and lay naked next to him.**

- If you intend to wait until marriage for sex, it's stupid to place yourself in precarious situations.

- ❖ **Not all men are the same.**

- ❖ Your current boyfriend shouldn't have to put up with unhealthy baggage from all your previous relationships.

- ❖ **It's wrong to let your husband think the baby is his when it really belongs to the dude you banged the night before your wedding.**

- ❖ Nice men are out there—you just can't see them because you are blinded by hurts from the past.

- ❖ **You have to let go of the past to move on.**

- ❖ Why are you fighting so hard to hold on to something or someone that's no good for you?

- ❖ **MUSIC: "HAVE YOU EVER REALLY LOVED A WOMAN" BY BRIAN ADAMS**

- ❖ Marriage doesn't curb a man's appetite for new women.

- Only dating married men is bad for your reputation.

- **If your boyfriend has cheated on you multiple times, marrying him isn't going to solve the problem.**

- If your partner has been cheating on you all through your relationship, what makes you think he's husband material?

- **Just because he's your lover doesn't mean he's your boyfriend.**

- Just because he's the father of your children doesn't mean he's the one you should marry. You should also probably stop having children with him.

- **With most men, what you see is what you get.**

- Even if you invite your boyfriend into the delivery room to watch you push out his son, that doesn't mean he's going to love or even be there for you or his child especially if he did not want a baby with you in the first place.

❖ **If your boyfriend tells you he doesn't want a baby, he's expecting you not to get pregnant, even though you allow him to have unprotected sex with you.**

❖ When some men make an agreement with you that is in their best interest, they expect you to stick to it. On the other hand, if said agreement is in your best interest those same men want you to be understanding if they break the terms of the agreement.

❖ **Pay attention to the mannerisms of your boyfriend as he might be on the down low.**

❖ It's foolish to knowingly marry a gay man thinking you can switch him over.

❖ **An unpleasant fact is when you leave through the front door, a man might be visiting your husband through the**

back door—literally and figuratively.

- A man is first attracted to your outer beauty; give him a chance to explore your inner beauty.

- **Some men don't mind buying you material things to get into your pants because it's part of their budget; however, they will probably not marry you after they have hit it, smacked it, flipped it, and rubbed it down.**

- As an older woman, you might be able to seduce a younger man, but you will never be able to control or keep up with him.

- If you are a woman in your forties or fifties with children dating a younger man without children, the relationship might not go anywhere.

- **As women, in your forties or fifties with**

teenage children, are you sure you want to marry a man in his twenties with no children?

❖ **As invigorating as it may seem to date younger men, you have to be wise and cautious.**

❖ It's unwise to already have teenage children practically off to college and then get pregnant again in your mid-forties to provide your young lover with children of his own.

❖ **No matter how good you look as a woman in your forties, fifties, or sixties, in the long run you will never be able to compete with a twenty-year-old woman with perky boobs.**

❖ As an older woman, you shouldn't try to compete with younger women; instead, mentor them, as some really need the guidance of an older more mature woman.

- ❖ **Some younger men simply want a cougar who thinks she's in control to pay for their extravagant lifestyles. They give you good sex and make you feel young again; in turn, you pay their rent. A nice quid pro quo arrangement.**

- ❖ The only reason men act the way they do is because of the women in their lives.

- ❖ **You enable his selfish behavior.**

- ❖ Teach him to walk instead of letting him run all over you.

- ❖ **If he did not nurture you after your miscarriage, why would you get pregnant for him again?**

- ❖ Pay attention to your boyfriend's relationship with his mother.

- **If a man has unhealthy relationships with the women in his family, that says a lot.**

- Pay attention to the way your boyfriend talks about women.

- If there's evidence of your boyfriend referring to women as bitches, what do you think he thinks of you? If you think you are the only woman he doesn't consider a bitch, you are delusional.

- **There are only two females a man doesn't consider bitches: his mother and his daughter.**

- Pay attention to the way your boyfriend treats children; if he's abrupt and intolerant of them, that could be a problem.

- **Take notice of your boyfriend's interaction with children because he might be pretending**

to like them in hopes you will think he will be a good husband and father.

❖ When it comes to men, you should listen more than you speak; save the gibberish for your girlfriends.

❖ **Some men are good at faking sanity; it's your responsibility to discover the insanity.**

❖ Sometimes it's difficult for a man to verbalize his feelings in a relationship, so pay attention to his actions.

❖ It's ill-advised to let anyone manipulate you into motherhood.

❖ **If there's no marriage certificate, he isn't your husband.**

❖ Unless you are married to a man, if anyt8ing happens to him, his mother is in charge.

❖ Stop beating up your boyfriend or spouse.

- **One of the reasons your husband would rather kill you than divorce you is the satisfaction of never hearing your voice again.**

- What goes around comes right back around and that is a fact.

- No matter what crimes a man has committed in his life, he will always be able to find a woman willing to marry him. You don't have that luxury.

- **Ain't nothing going on but the rent; make sure yours is paid.**

- Not all your friends give good advice; weed out the ones who do not.

- **"When a man loves you, he takes care of you in life and in death." – Read Wikipedia about King**

Leopard II of Belgium and <u>Caroline Lacroix</u>

❖ Abortion isn't birth control.

❖ **Technically an abortion isn't a miscarriage.**

❖ Abortion is a physical act, but it can take you years to mentally recover.

❖ **Why put your body through an abortion for a man who doesn't think you are valuable enough to marry?**

❖ If you tell your boyfriend that you are pregnant and he asks what *you* are going to do, he's telling you what to do.

❖ If you are good enough to sleep with, you are good enough to marry.

❖ **You determine who you want to be in a relationship: sex slave,**

girlfriend, wife, mistress, or mistake.

- ❖ It's reckless to put your body through back-alley abortions only to marry the man of your dreams and be unable to bear him a child.

- ❖ Do you honestly think he cares about you if he's demanding an abortion?

❖ An abortion should be your choice.

- ❖ The same man who says, "Ooh baby it feels so much better without a condom," and with whom you are having unprotected sex, is the same man that will refuse to marry you and is voting against abortions.

❖ Bottom line: If you don't ever want to be in a situation where you have to consider an abortion, keep your legs closed until you marry a decent man (not for rape and molestation victims).

- There are different types of abuse: verbal, physical, and psychological.

- **You belong to a league of extraordinary women.**

- When a person is in love with you, all you need is a beating heart.

- You do yourself no favors by marrying a man who is in love with another woman.

- **Very few men do things for women they don't like or women they aren't having sex with.**

- The ultimate goal of most men is to either get you down on your knees or on your back as soon as possible.

- **Stop being so hard on yourself and learn to make peace with your *past* poor decisions.**

- Everyone experiences failures; learn from yours and move on.

- ❖ **A man has to do what a man has to do…BABY.**

- ❖ If you have been dating a man since your twenties and are currently in your late thirties, and he isn't interested in getting married or having children as you have been for the last fifteen years, it's time to cut your losses and move on.

- ❖ **As a woman with limited time and marriage and babies on your mind, you can't afford decade-long relationships without marital commitment.**

- ❖ One of the reasons he likes you so much is because you are not that bright, and he can do as he pleases in the relationship without any objection from you.

- ❖ Treat yourself to a solo vacation at least once in your lifetime.

- ❖ **It's imprudent to ignore your biological clock, but don't obsess about it**

either—all the children you are meant to have, you will have.

- You don't need a man to have fun but it's more fun when they are around.

- When traveling alone, be mindful of your surroundings.

- **A friends with benefits situation is mostly beneficial for him.**

- One of the reasons a man wants a friends with benefits situation with you is because you don't make the cut for being his girlfriend; however, you have a hot body and are stupid enough to believe hot sex on a platter will eventually make him your boyfriend.

- **It's very difficult for most woman to detach emotions from sex.**

- It's unwise to stifle your growth because of the relationship you are in.

- ❖ **Hold your partner or spouse accountable for his or her actions.**

- ❖ It's unwise to marry a man whose decisions you can't influence.

- ❖ **READ: "YOUR KNIGHT IN SHINING ARMOR: DISCOVERING YOUR LIFELONG LOVE" BY P. B. WILSON**

- ❖ Those shoes are made for walking; know when to walk away from a bad romance.

- ❖ **Just because you are afraid of your husband doesn't mean other women are afraid of him too.**

- ❖ Take a salsa or meringue class just for the heck of it.

- ❖ **MUSIC: "MAN, I FEEL LIKE A WOMAN" BY SHANIA TWAIN**

- Date and/or marry a man who makes you feel like a woman.

- Date and marry a man who can teach you something enlightening about life.

- **It's life threatening to be a whiny, nagging, complaining girlfriend or wife, or you might end up at the bottom of the Hudson River.**

- The judicial system primarily recognizes marriage certificates, not shacking up arrangements.

- Keep your parents as your beneficiaries on your life insurance policy because you never know when you might accidentally fall from a bridge while hiking with your new husband.

- **You have to be careful of the man you marry because he might only be marrying you for your life insurance policy.**

❖ **If your husband physically abuses you, call the police and file charges—even if he claims to love you or if he's a celebrity.**

❖ Some jail time might help bring an abusive man to his senses, but don't stick around to find out.

❖ If he hits you once, he's more than likely to keep hitting you.

❖ **The first punch from a man is sometimes the feeler punch to see how you will react. If you don't do anything, you will more than likely keep feeling punches.**

❖ Some men are indeed women beaters, and some just need a woman to send them to the emergency room once.

❖ **You set a bad example for your child18en if**

you stay in an abusive relationship.

- If you are miserable in your single life, you will more than likely be miserable in your married life too.

- **Marriage doesn't solve the problem of feeling lonely and unloved.**

- Learn to be happy in your single life before getting married.

- Marriage doesn't solve problems.

- **Even with all your love and understanding, you will never be able to change your boyfriend.**

- If your boyfriend is a crack head, you are more than likely not going to get him off crack; if anything, he's going to get you on crack.

- **Most women usually follow the lead of the men they are in relationships with, so**

choose a good/decent one.

❖ You can invite a man to church, but you can't make him stay and be baptized.

❖ **There are some scoundrels in your church; be cautious.**

❖ Either he wants to be part of the church or not; you can't save him.

❖ Don't be fooled by the rocks that he has because they could be borrowed, stolen, or rented.

❖ **There's something to be said for not allowing yourself to be unevenly yoked.**

❖ It's foolish to treat women like your enemies; instead, treat them like your friends.

❖ Be passionate and optimistic about your future.

❖ **Your best days are in front of you, and**

hopefully the worst are behind.

- It's reckless to get hypnotized by a charismatic pastor, preacher, or evangelist.

- **It's a bad idea to meet up with your married Bible talk leader after hours.**

- **Single, saved, and having sex is good for him, but what happens if you get pregnant?**

- Single, saved, and pregnant—you should still go to church.

- **Cheating doesn't have to be physical; it can also be emotional.**

- Just because he takes really good care of you doesn't mean he isn't cheating on you.

- What man of God has sexual relations with anyone but his wife?

- ❖ **Know the word of God for yourself, and don't allow your spouse to m1nipulate you with it.**

- ❖ Men of the cloth are not infallible.

- ❖ **Men are afraid of three things: other men, death, and their schlongs falling off.**

- ❖ The only pain some men feel is that of a physical nature.

- ❖ No sex tapes with boyfriends.

- ❖ **If you are stupid enough to make a sex tape with your boyfriend and then sell it, don't be surprised if your character is always called into question.**

- ❖ It's ill-advised to waste your time fantasizing about the life you want; instead, work tirelessly to make it happen.

- **Worshipping a man as if he's your god will eventually bring you out of your stupor.**

- Most men don't believe you when you say, "This has never happened before."

- Smart men know the difference between a whore and a housewife.

- Most men will bang a promiscuous woman but the majority of them won't marry one especially if she has a reputation.

- **Under no circumstances should you ever say to a man, "I am down for whatever, whenever, wherever."**

- The only man you should think about being an adventurous freak for is the one who put a ring on your finger—after he signs the marriage certificate.

- **Most men usually don't buy the cow if they can**

milk you whenever and wherever they choose.

❖ Make the best of your younger years so you are not bitter in your older days.

❖ **Don't pass down bitterness from one generation to another.**

❖ It's reckless to pass over the nice guy with ambition for a crook with a Bentley.

❖ It's not recommended to marry your second choice only to abuse him or her.

❖ **Just because a man left his wife for you doesn't mean it's OK to flaunt your relationship in her face.**

❖ The grass always looks greener on the other side until you get over there and realize its fake grass.

❖ **Relationships require a lot of give and take; make plans to have only**

85 percent of what you want.

- It's foolish to trade in an 85 percent for a 15 percent.

- **In your relationship, you had better know which side of the bread your butter is on, meaning, it's unwise to dump your hardworking spouse for a person who offers good sex and can't afford to take care of you and your children if your spouse kicks you out on your fanny.**

- If you have four children by three different men and have never been married, you can't afford to window-shop when it comes to schlongs.

- Some husbands have no intention of letting you return home safely from your vacation.

- **If you have had multiple abortions, it's time to put the schlong down.**

- Men are creatures of habit.

- When it comes to men, timing is everything.

- **Learn to rescue yourself from the big bad wolf.**

- It is reckless to marry a man your children are afraid of.

- Some married men are always looking for a little extra on the side; don't be that extra!

- **Most married men don't intend to ever leave their wives for you, no matter what they say.**

- Your birth control is your problem, and his birth control is *also* your problem.

- **If you are a good Catholic girl and don't want to have an abortion**

or an illegitimate child, don't have unprotected sex.

- If you are sleeping with your boyfriend, your birth control should be part of his budget, and if he's paying for it, you should take it.

- Take yourself on a date at least once a month.

❖ Going dutch on a date is a major faux pas.

- The only dutch you should acknowledge is Dutch Schultz.

❖ Depending on the man you go on a date with, if you order lobster, he might be expecting breakfast in the morning.

- Save all that good sex for your husband.

- Hot sex on a platter doesn't keep a man.

❖ Save something special for your husband.

- There are actually some men who are intrigued and fascinated by your thoughts.

- **The length of the schlong showing through his biker shorts doesn't make him marriage material.**

- Most men need to feel useful so find things around the house that you need him to do besides you.

- **Let him take out the trash.**

- You are not supposed to cook, do the dishes, wash the bathroom, and do his laundry by default.

- **As your husband, he should make sure all your needs are taken care of.**

- A married woman should never have to borrow money from friends.

- What is up with you acting like a wife when you and your boyfriend have never discussed marriage?

- **You can be still be discovered by a decent man if you are divorced with three children.**

- It's better to be single and happy than married and depressed.

- **Pay attention to your husband's patterns; that is to say, if he has six children with four other women and isn't taking care of any of them, there's a possibility that you might end up raising your children on your own.**

- Some men don't want women who will help to make them better; instead, they prefer women who will do as they say.

- **As a wise wife, you will at times need to be the intermediary for your unwise husband.**

- Bad boys are fun in your twenties but an absolute nightmare in your thirties.

- **There are many stupid and lovelorn women in jail; it's foolish to be one of them.**

- If you are responsible for the family finances, be wise with your spending.

- **Love him, but love you more.**

- Live and love your life—you only get one chance to make the best of it.

- **Live, love, laugh, and love a little bit harder.**

- **At the end of the day, most men are going to marry a lady.**

- Most men don't know how to recognize a respectable woman until their friend marries one.

- **If you just got out of another bad relationship, you have to take responsibility for your actions in that and all your previous relationships because that is the only way to move on without feeling bitter.**

- Decide whether you want him for a season or a lifetime, and then act accordingly. Your actions will determine the results.

- **If you don't have any DNA connection to a man, he considers you bangable.**

- If you continuously date clowns, someone is always going to be laughing, and it will not be you.

- The concept of getting and trying to keep a man is destructive.

- **It's honorable and healthy to live your life with your legs crossed until marriage.**

- When a man dumps you, sometimes it's in your best interest.

- **If there's no marriage certificate and you are pregnant, *you are having a baby*.**

- You are stronger and more empowering than you know.

- **Being an empowering woman doesn't have to be defined by in-your-face sexuality.**

- **There's nothing wrong with owning your sexuality, but exploiting it and calling it empowering is delusional.**

- Just because a man isn't ill-treating you doesn't mean he did not physically abuse his ex-girlfriend.

- **Truth be told, one woman can bring out the best in one man and the worst in another.**

- No matter what, men always come out on top.

- Sometimes, it's best to let men deal with men.

- **It's not recommended to let a man spoil you with his money and material items because that will only keep you financially dependent upon him.**

- Try to provide yourself with the finer things in life, so if your rich boyfriend dumps you, you are still able to enjoy these things.

- Some rich douche bags treat dependent and independent women very differently.

❖ Don't be stupid and let your boyfriend con you into killing his wife so you can be together because when everything unravels, and you are convicted of her murder, he will be on to the next woman before the judge pounds his gravel to conclude your trial.

❖ **It's foolish to let a man use you to get rid of his problematic wife.**

❖ If you prefer dating married men, something is definitely wrong with you.

❖ **If you are married with no children and want to stay uninvolved with what is going on financially in your household, that is fine. However, when you start having children, it's your responsibility as a caring mother to know what is going on because if your husband decides to dump you,**

you and your children are screwed.

❖ If you are a stay-at-home mother, it's risky to stay out of the workforce for too many years.

❖ **Love in its true form is beautiful and divine.**

❖ There's a season for everything including babies, but not when you are broke living from paycheck to paycheck.

❖ **It's OK to think of a man as a prince until he opens his mouth.**

❖ You shouldn't mimic the bad behaviors of the men in your life.

❖ **The "If men do it, why can't women do it?" mentality is destructive.**

❖ Men are men and women are women; both have different roles to play and when those roles become blurred, confusion ensues.

- **The same privileges offered to a husband shouldn't be offered to a boyfriend.**

- **Your boyfriend or husband should enhance your life spiritually.**

- Choose a man with heart because it sucks to have a boyfriend who is a punk.

- A little sexting between husband and wife is harmless.

- **When was the last time you held your husband just to hold him.**

- The main reason your scumbag ex-boyfriend wants to meet up after dumping you is to gloat about his so-called wonderful life. But if it's so wonderful, why does he feel the need to brag about it?

- **Even though all might seem well with your abusive ex-boyfriend,**

never allow yourself to feel guilty for dumping him.

❖ You and your abusive ex-boyfriend or ex-husband should never ever get back together.

❖ **To divide and conquer, some men look for the weakest link. Don't be the weakest link.**

❖ Never give a man the satisfaction by hearing you ask, "Why not me?"

❖ **If your boyfriend makes a sex tape with you, your father should force him to marry you by standing behind him with a shotgun.**

❖ Most men don't do things for free, not even Christian men.

❖ **If you are a Christian woman being physically abused by your**

Christian husband from Monday to Saturday—but not on Sunday because God rested on Sundays—seek professional help.

- Before a man is anything (Christian, president, African American, Caucasian, judge, teacher, pilot, athlete, evangelist, etc.,), he's a man, and he needs some sexual healing from his wife.

- **Just because you have a high-power job doesn't mean it's advisable to be away from your sexually charged husband for too many days or weeks. If you do, you can't be surprised when he gets in trouble by lurking around Twitter and/or Facebook looking for companionship.**

***
Men

- **You should act like the prince you rightfully are instead of accepting pauper status.**

- If you survived growing up and out of the projects, go back to mentor a child just like you.

- **You deserve to be with a woman who loves and respects you both in and out of the bedroom.**

- It's disrespectful to disrespect the mother of your children.

- **If your mother is disrespectful to your wife, have a serious conversation with your mother!**

- Just because you have a wife now doesn't mean you should become unimaginative in the bedroom.

- **One of the reasons your wife loves the *Fifty Shades of Grey* series so much might have something to do with you.**

- How and when did God reveal that your girlfriend should become your wife?

- It's your fault if you marry a woman who doesn't love you.

- **Marry the girl you love, even though her reputation might not be good for your career or social status.**

- Do yourself a tremendous favor and marry a woman who is sharp because marrying a dim-witted one will cost you more in the end.

- Always defend the reputation of your wife but don't be stupid or ignorant about it.

- It's rash to marry a woman who is a gold digger because when your gold disappears so will she.

- ### If you are unemployed, you can't afford to have sex.

- Refrain from using your money to get, keep, or control a woman.

- ### It's no surprise that she got pregnant. It was predetermined from the first date when you were stupid enough to believe her when she said, "Don't worry about it, I am on the pill."

- Ideally, you shouldn't sleep with anyone you don't want to have children with; after all, accidents do happen.

- Only a loser uses money to get women.

- How can you expect a woman to want to get to know you for who you are when you keep distracting her with material merchandise? Money can't buy love.

- ### Treat the women in your life with nuff respect.

- Some women simply don't know how to value a good man.

- **Some women don't know how to appreciate a good man until they meet one who treats them badly.**

- If your wife doesn't want to have a baby with you, she probably doesn't feel comfortable with you.

- **Not all women want to be married with children and you might be married to one.**

- If you don't intend to marry her, let her go.

- Your girlfriend is probably more emotional than you are, so be careful how you treat her.

- **No matter how strong she is, she still needs a great big hug from you occasionally.**

- ❖ Beware of the cherry pie woman. This is a type of woman who is at a stage in her life where she wants to get married and have children, so she acts the way she thinks you want her to act and let you put *it* anywhere, but as soon as the ring goes on and the babies are born her real character surfaces and its usually not so pretty.

- ❖ **Hand-write a love letter to your ladylove occasionally.**

- ❖ Why are you infatuated with women who don't seem to know you exist?

- ❖ **What is a nice guy like you doing with a monster like her?**

- ❖ There should only be one person wearing the pants in your relationship, and it should be you.

- ❖ If you are afraid of your woman, you are a punk.

- ❖ **Always open the door for a woman—even an ungrateful one.**

- Single, saved, and having sex, what happens if she gets pregnant?

- **Align yourself with men who inspire you.**

- Instead of being jealous of your colleague's successes, celebrate them with him.

- It's ill-advised to let a woman come between you and your friends, unless she's your wife.

- There are more productive ways to deal with conflicts than with your fists.

- **Other men treat you according to how you act; if you act like a punk, they will treat you as such.**

- Never fight a person that isn't as attractive as you are.

- **Consistently work on your character rather than your biceps.**

- You deserve to be in a loving and nurturing relationship.

- You can always find a woman who will worship the ground you walk on.

- **No means no even if she's naked in your bed.**

- There's nothing wrong with being a sensitive man.

- **Before you marry a woman, think about what kind of mother she will be.**

- Instead of marrying a woman who only meets your needs, think about your future children.

- Not all women will make good mothers.

- **A woman doesn't have to be a beauty queen to be a good wife and an excellent mother.**

- Don't let your desire for exotic-looking babies cloud your judgment when it comes to an exotic-looking crazy chick.

- Don't get distracted by her beauty because she might actually be a psychotic beauty.

❖ CLASSIC TUNE: "SORRY" BY FOXY BROWN (REGGAE VERSION)

❖ There are other ways to provide for your family without selling drugs.

❖ **It's felonious to waste a woman's time if you know she isn't the one.**

❖ If you are a rich guy and your girlfriend gets pregnant and decides to keep the baby, pay your child support instead of hiring a hit man to kill her. It's not worth it to spend the next twenty-four years of your life in jail.

❖ **Just because a woman comes across as unassuming doesn't mean she isn't crazy.**

❖ If you work at McDonald's or United Parcel Service (UPS) earning a respectable living, you are admired more than drug dealers.

❖ Making an honest day's pay working at Home Depot isn't something to be ashamed of.

- You set the tone of your relationship.

- **If your girlfriend doesn't trust you, you are sometimes partly to blame.**

- If your girlfriend is uncomfortable with you being friends with an ex-lover on Facebook—acknowledge, respect, and do something about it.

- **Your girlfriend doesn't have to obey you; who do you think you are?**

- It's risky to pack your bags to follow some chick overseas unless she's the one.

- It's best not to put your life on hold for anyone.

- What exactly is a promise ring?

- **Stop wasting your money on seasonal women, and save it to spend on the one you want for a lifetime.**

- If you want to get married, start saving for the ring and a house to put your wife in.

- Save part of yourself for your wife that no other woman has ever experienced.

❖ MUSIC: "GOOD MAN" BY RAPHAEL SAADIQ

❖ A good woman can take you to heights you have never been before, so choose wisely.

- It's better to divorce your wife than to kill her.

- It might be cheaper to keep her, but your happiness is priceless.

- It might be cheaper to keep her, but are you sure you want to keep her?

❖ If you know yourself, you know which woman is best for you.

- Stop leading on your best friend.

❖ **Most of the bad situations you get yourself into with women result from your recklessness.**

❖ You are asking for trouble if you cheat on your girlfriend in her apartment.

❖ If it was not you banging the next-door neighbor on the sofa, who was it?

❖ **If you don't want to have children with a woman, why are you having sex with her?**

❖ Always use protection, regardless of what your girlfriend or boyfriend says.

❖ It's unbeneficial to attempt to force your girlfriend to have an abortion.

❖ **Some men don't understand that an abortion is more than a physical act; it's also**

extremely emotional and traumatic. Don't be one of those insensitive jerks.

- It can take a lifetime for a woman to emotionally recover from an abortion.

- **Abortions are uncool, but you have no right to tell a woman what she can and can't do with her body, especially if you are unwilling to make an honest woman out of her.**

- You are sloppy if you have had many women have abortions on account of you.

- How can you expect your spouse to treat you like a man when you act like a man-child?

- **You are the best.**

- Monogamy is still admirable and healthy.

- If you don't think you can be faithful to your girlfriend, leave her alone.

- **Learn to develop genuine friendships with women.**

- Not all your friendships with women need to involve sex.

- If you don't want to be in a relationship with a woman, stop having sex with her.

- **Some women equate sex with love.**

- Thank you for all the hugs.

- **No matter what anyone says, you have potential.**

- Learn to cook.

- Women love a good dancer.

- **Instead of being charming, be yourself.**

- Respect your relationship by respecting yourself.

- ❖ Try to be an admirable role model for the young men in your life.

- ❖ **Dinner and a movie are unimaginative and downright lazy for a first date.**

- ❖ Not every man can be rich and famous, but every man has the potential to be an outstanding husband, provider, father, and lover.

- ❖ Know your strengths and weaknesses.

- ❖ **Marry the woman who uplifts you, not the one who tears you down.**

- ❖ Underage girls are trouble.

- ❖ Just because a woman acts like a whore doesn't mean you should to treat her like one.

- ❖ **When you favor a sperm depository over a virtuous woman, you deserve the *good* life.**

- It's OK to want many women but marry the one you need and be faithful unto her.

- **If your wife cheats on you, you should offer her the same mercy you would like if the shoe was on the other foot.**

- A promiscuous person is disgusting and potentially infectious.

- Get tested for HIV consistently.

- Think with your north head instead of your south head.

- **The only reason you want a friends with benefits relationship with a woman is because she isn't girlfriend material but is a warm body and is stupid enough to let you have sex with her whenever in hopes that one day you'll be her boyfriend.**

But you already know this…wink, wink!

❖ Don't use a woman's stupidity against her.

❖ **Sleeping with your friend's, teammate's, or boss's wife is a no-no.**

❖ Just because someone gave you a sexually transmitted disease (STD) doesn't mean you should give it to as many people as possible.

❖ **Not all women are the same.**

❖ If you attract the same type of women, do some self-evaluation.

❖ **If your woman physically abuses you, call the cops—even if you are six foot seven and weigh 330 pounds, and she's five foot two and weighs one hundred pounds.**

- ❖ You should never hit a woman.

- ❖ **If you are crazy in love with a crazy woman who beats you, you are crazy.**

- ❖ There's a difference between loving and respecting your mother and being a mama's boy.

- ❖ It's embarrassing and hurtful when your wife has to go through your mother to get to you.

- ❖ **Being a good father starts long before your little soldier fertilizes the egg.**

- ❖ Be the father you never had.

- ❖ **If your father was not in your life, at some point God is going to give you an opportunity to be a father; show him you are a better man than your father was.**

- Don't complain about your father abandoning you and then turn around and do the same to your children.

- If you only have daughters, take it up with God and not your wife.

- **Using and abusing women will come back to you in the form of a daughter.**

- What kind of man lets a woman pay his bills?

- If a woman is paying your bills, she's going to try to control you.

- **It's criminal to sleep with married women because someone might sleep with your wife.**

- Don't say to your mistress, "The man who marries you is going to be a lucky man."

- **A good woman is priceless; choose wisely.**

- A family member disrespecting your wife is unacceptable.

- Strive to be a man worthy of the calling you have been offered.

- Your actions speak louder than your words.

- **Your actions should coincide with your words.**

- Be honest about your financial situation with your partner.

- **If you can't afford her expensive taste, let her know. Don't rob a bank trying to get her these things.**

- How can you expect her to know you when you don't know yourself?

- Teach your significant other how to love you the right way.

- Some women offer you food to ensnare you.

- **It's gluttonous and unwise to accept food from anyone but your spouse.**

- ❖ **Some women change after marriage for the better.**

  - ❖ Be there when your wife is having your baby.

  - ❖ All your children should have your surname.

- ❖ **It's unwise to cheat on your spouse to get his or her attention.**

  - ❖ Talk about your feelings.

  - ❖ Occasionally, let it out—crying is masculine, but bawling is not.

- ❖ **There's nothing wrong with being a Godly man.**

  - ❖ Never use a baby to try to trap a woman.

  - ❖ Cheating, even if done respectfully, is still wrong.

- ❖ **In the same way you mistreat a woman, another man will do the**

same to your daughter. What will you do then?

❖ If you refer to women as bitches and whores, don't be surprised when your princess brings home someone just like you.

❖ You can try to hide your past from your children, but you can't hide the repercussions.

❖ If you like freaky activities, marry a woman who feels the same way instead of a prude, or you will more than likely end up cheating on her with a super freak.

❖ Marry someone who can keep up with your sexual appetite.

❖ Some women might take on manly roles, but they still want to be romanced like women.

❖ Why is it your child's mother is the only one raising your children?

- If you are having marital problems, the hot double-jointed intern isn't the best person to be hanging out with.

- Cheating starts as lust and then manifests.

- **Don't underestimate the power of your lustful heart especially if you don't make an effort to control it.**

- You don't have to succumb to the corruption of your heart.

- **If you are sixty-five years old and a billionaire, and she's twenty-five years old—what is the probability she's in it for love?**

- Just because you are married to a Christian woman does not mean you are the lord of her universe.

- ❖ **Using the Bible to manipulate and rebuke your wife will not produce a long and healthy marriage.**

- ❖ Your children are paying attention to the kind of man you are inside and outside the church.

- ❖ Giving a girl a framed picture of yourself in your boxers is clownish.

- ❖ **No woman is out of your league.**

- ❖ A spiritual man is irresistible, so make an effort to be one.

- ❖ If you were born a man and still have the equipment, but are currently living as a woman, let the men you date know before it's too late.

- ❖ **It doesn't matter how rich or popular you are; if you are not taking care of all your children, you are a scumbag.**

- Nothing is wrong with making sure the baby is yours before you start paying child support.

- If after fifteen years, you discover that your child isn't your biological child, it's unfair to the child to simply walk away.

- Being able to grow with someone is essential for a healthy, long-lasting relationship.

- **Sam Cooke, Stevie Wonder, Bing Crosby, Donny Hathaway, Marvin Gaye, Al Green, The Four Tops, Vic Damone, Earth, Wind & Fire, Perry Como, The Isley Brothers, Lionel Richie / The Commodores, Bobby Darin, Kool & the Gang, Kenny Rogers, Hall & Oates, Lou Rawls, Luther Vandross, Buddy Clark, The O'Jays, Barry White, The Spinners, Phil Collins, Frank Sinatra,**

Boyz II Men, Julio Iglesias, **R. Kelly**, Bobby Womack, **Roger Whittaker**, Michael Bolton, **The Temptations**, Main Ingredient, **The Chi-Lites**, Marc Anthony, **The Staple Singers, The Stylistics**, Richard Marx, **Bill Withe18s**, Babyface, **Eddie Fisher**, Maxwell, **Peabo Bryson**, Billy Joel, **James Ingram**, Frankie Valli, **Rod Stewart, and** Teddy Pendergrass **are your friends.**

CHAPTER 8

POP CULTURE

***
<u>Introduction</u>

Pop culture, pop culture, pop culture. I'm seriously at a loss for words.

Some of it is really good and entertaining while other parts are bewildering and vacuous at best.

As I sit back and observe the evolution of pop culture I'm mystified by some of the observations I've made.

POP CULTURE

* * *

- Pop culture is entertaining.

- Keeping track of pop culture is time-consuming.

- **Not everything on the Internet is true.**

- It's unproductive to allow yourself to be consumed by pop culture.

- Without the 99 percent, there would be no 1 percent.

- **If you want to pay little or no taxes, become part of the 1 percent.**

- Low taxes are one of the benefits of being rich.

- You shouldn't buy a gadget that costs more than your rent.

- **Abortion is a woman's issue.**

- Some men are against abortions until their mistresses need them.

- Some politicians fundamentally believe, "Do as I say, but not as I do."

- **Politicians are masters at practicing honne in private and tatemae in public.**

- Corruption in public service exists mainly because it's tolerated at higher levels.

- **Most congressional hearings are acts of posturing.**

- The world has too much politics but not enough policies.

- **Why can't we get rid of politics, and instead do the right thing?**

- **A political organization can't be deemed incorruptible when it is made up of corruptible people.**

- If you don't vote, you can't complain... at all.

- Regardless of what you think, your vote counts for more than you know.

- **If you don't want to vote for yourself, vote for your disenfranchised ancestors who paved the way.**

- Instead of keeping track of pop culture at work, you should actually be ~~working~~.

- More and more, bad publicity is turning into good publicity.

- **If you are famous, it's very easy to manipulate the media.**

- A celebrity might not be the best person to emulate.

- **PEOPLE: BOB MARLEY**

- Bob Marley isn't only an alleged ganja smoker but also a brilliant musical artist.

- ❖ **It is OK to be skinny while single, but when you get married, you should be juicy.**

- ❖ If your marriage is on the rocks, reality television isn't for you.

- ❖ Learning Adobe Photoshop and Illustrator is a beneficial side hustle.

- ❖ **READ: "THE HEROIN DIARIES: A YEAR IN THE LIFE OF A SHATTERED ROCK STAR" BY NIKKI SIXX**

- ❖ Messing around with any type of drug is the beginning of a bad romance, and *you will* be slaughtered.

- ❖ Drugs will not only kill you, but they can devastate your family for generations to come.

- ❖ **Being addicted to drugs is like standing on the train tracks thinking you have the ability to**

stop the oncoming train from running you over.

- So what if a politician cheats on his wife? That is between them.

- The next time a politician cheats on his wife, he should say, "I am an imperfect man living in an imperfect world, but this is between me and my wife, and we would appreciate some privacy."

- **Political ideology should be consistently evolving and being amended.**

- If your company keeps hiring the same people from the same background to do the same job, you will continue to get the same results.

- **Positive change doesn't necessarily come about voluntarily.**

- Change does take time especially if your administration is continuously being filibustered.

- **The people who amend the laws are the same people who benefit most from those amendments.**

- The people who amend the laws do so knowing fully how to get around them.

- **MUSIC: THE BEATLES**

- When is the British royal family going to culturally mix things up? They all look the same...boring.

- **Some politicians have personal agendas that have nothing to do with the interests of the public.**

- Most politicians are corruptible just like most human beings.

- **Believe marginally what politicians say.**

- It's not that some politicians don't want to fulfill the promises they made on the campaign trail, it's just that they tend to overreach.

- **Guns and alcohol make punks brave.**

- Violence in movies isn't the problem—people are.

- **Just because you didn't pull the trigger doesn't mean you are absolved of any responsibility.**

- Instead of criminalizing ganja smokers, why don't politicians go after people who are distributing illegal guns?

- **It's unwise to simply believe what people tell you; instead, do your own research.**

- Make sure you have all the facts before joining the conversation.

GOOD|BAD: WIKILEAKS

- Just because for most of your life you have been treated unfairly doesn't mean you shouldn't fight for the rights of others.

- **Broaden your horizons by broadening your understanding of life.**

- Life is too short to visit the same place twice.

- **Know your rights as a citizen of the world.**

- Be knowledgeable about what is going on in the world and not just your community.

- Knowledge puffs up but love builds up.

- **Ninety percent of the people who you think are thinking about you don't know you exist.**

- Pop culture isn't what it used to be.

- The quality of music has diminished over time.

- **Wild animals belong in the wild, so don't be surprised when they go wild on you.**

- If you have a pet ape, feeding it wine and treating it like your boyfriend is bananas.

- One of the reasons your animal is so vicious probably has to do with you feeding it raw meat daily.

- **No matter what you think, your pet isn't on the same level as human beings.**

- If you don't have a leash for your ferocious fifty-pound pit bull, keep it locked in your basement.

- **People in the suburbs pay a bundle to live in peace and quiet and not be jolted awake at 1:00 a.m. by loud music or fireworks.**

- Somewhere out there, someone is thinking of you in a loving way.

❖ **The media should be objective instead of subjective.**

  ❖ What happened to investigative reporting?

❖ **Two and a Half Men episodes with Charlie Sheen are golden.**

  ❖ Charlie Harper's lifestyle shouldn't be imitated.

  ❖ Love in the movies is different from love in real life.

❖ **Does art imitate life or does life imitate art?**

  ❖ Real life is better than fiction.

  ❖ Pop stars are for entertainment, not imitation.

❖ **It's sad when class wants to future generations to imitate crass.**

  ❖ It's misguided to try to imitate the lives of celebrities because what you see isn't always realistic.

- Not all women are angels, and not all men are demons.

- If you think wearing a crucifix around your neck makes you a Christian, you are kidding yourself.

- **Some people's heads are so far up their arses that they can't see the value in the common person.**

- No matter how pretty the package, trash is still trash.

- **Look closer to home for role models than the pages of magazines.**

- No matter what a magazine cover says there's no kind of sex that will make a man stay…unless he wants to.

- You shouldn't try to look like people on magazine covers because they don't look like that in real life.

❖ WATCH: GUY CODE

- Social media is good for keeping in touch with long-lost friends; however, it is not good for stalking ex-lovers.

- ❖ **Keep yourself marketable by keeping up with new technology.**

- ❖ Stop wasting your time stalking celebrities on the Internet; instead, get a life.

- ❖ No one likes a wannabe.

- ❖ **It's ill-advised to befriend your boss on social media if you are a disgruntled employee talking trash.**

- ❖ Other nationalities besides African American women wear extensions.

- ❖ The National Basketball Association (NBA) was at its peak in the 1990s.

- ❖ **Mind your own business 95 percent of the time.**

- ❖ There's a way to get involved while still minding your business.

- ❖ Most award shows are drab.

- ❖ **Watch television in small increments.**

- ❖ Meet up with your friends periodically to see how they are *really* doing.

- ❖ **Pick up the phone and call a friend instead of always texting him or her.**

- ❖ **MEMORABLE LINE: "ARE YOU GOING TO BELIEVE WHAT I TELL YOU OR WHAT YOUR LYING EYES SEE?" (MAN CAUGHT CHEATING ON GIRLFRIEND)**

- ❖ What is up with piercing baby boys' ears?

- ❖ Body piercings help to heighten sensitivity.

- ❖ **Under no circumstances should you get your lover's name tattooed on your body.**

- Most women have tattoos; they are called stretch marks.

- **The mockery of God in pop culture is sacrilegious.**

- Better to say, "I don't want to live by God's standards" than, "There's no God."

- **Wikipedia is your friend; donate at least $25 annually.**

- Everyone is entitled to an I don't care day—just don't abuse the privilege.

- Reggae music and sprinting should be left to Jamaicans.

- **MUSIC: "JAMAICAN IN NEW YORK" BY SHINEHEAD**

- **PLACE: JAMAICA**

- **SCANDALOUS: CATHOLIC SEX ABUSE SCANDAL**

- As of 2012, the Catholic church has allegedly paid out over $2 billion to the families of children who have been sexually abused by priests.

- **Smoking, texting, and driving simultaneously might be convenient for you, but inconvenient for the life you might take.**

- Men are gradually morphing into women.

- Women are becoming stronger and men weaker.

- What is up with men referring to their girlfriends and wives as bitches?

- <u>**Urban Dictionary**</u> **is a fun website to visit for the latest terminology on pop culture.**

- When you run into a celebrity, give him or her space.

- **Become an Amazon Affiliate or Seller to**

make a little extra cha-ching on the side.

- ❖ Affiliate Marketing is a very progressive and lucrative career path.

- ❖ One of the reasons some African Americans celebrated the verdict of the O. J. Simpson trial was because finally in America an African American man was able to buy his freedom.

❖ WATCH: INTERVENTION ON A&E

- ❖ Hate the game...not the player.

- ❖ Hate to break it to you, but it is a quid pro quo world.

❖ EVENT: COLUMBINE HIGH SCHOOL MASSACRE

- ❖ Never pull over on a dark and lonely road because you hear police sirens.

- ❖ Getting married is still a respectable thing to do.

- **Celebrities are entitled to some semblance of privacy.**

- Masturbating while high on cough syrup is mind-blowing.

- **Why do celebrities complain about the paparazzi then turn around and sell their wedding photos?**

- Some paparazzi are out of control.

- **There are tons of spiritual lessons buried in <u>Kung Fu Panda</u> (2008).**

- So sick and tired of prequels, sequels, and reboots—where is the originality of Hollywood?

- **If you are dating a celebrity, respect his or her privacy by learning to keep your mouth shut** concerning the relationship.

- Get a smartphone primarily for functionality rather than looks.

- The advancement of women in the field of technology is a beaut9ful thing.

- **DOCUMENTARY: FREAKONOMICS (2005)**

- Numbers matter.

- Keep guns out of your home, especially if you have children.

- **Teachers carrying guns into classrooms isn't going to solve the problem of school shootings.**

- **Violence + Violence = More Violence**

- Autocorrect can get you in hot water.

- If you have expensive gadgets, keep them out of the reach of children.

❖ SCANDALOUS: PENN STATE SEX ABUSE CASE

- There should be more diversity in primetime television.

- If you use Botox, it should only be in small doses.

- **Nice guys might finish in the bathroom, but at least they finish.**

- Standing up to the bully in your life can be extremely empowering.

❖ DOCUMENTARY: OUTRAGE (2009)

- Racism, ageism, and sexism should have been left in the twentieth century.

❖ GOOD|BAD: EUGENICS

- There's no such thing as the master race.

❖ **The end of the world is upon us, but today isn't the day.**

❖ There are some people who would rather go naked than wear fur and those same people believe in having abortions—bewildering to some but understandable as people have different vices.

❖ The best speeches are the ones given from the heart.

❖ **REALITY OF THE SITUATION: <u>IT'S A MAN'S WORLD</u>...FOR NOW.**

❖ Declutter your inbox—and your life.

❖ Corporate America is treacherous, so prepare yourself.

❖ **Lust for money and power can make any ambitious person corruptible.**

❖ If you are determined to get it all, you might end up destroying yourself in the process.

- **The US government facilitates Wall Street.**

- Corporate America isn't for the faint of heart.

- **MYSTERY: D. B. COOPER**

- The results of the Milgram experiment are still relevant today.

- Going to an Ivy League college makes some people professionally lazy.

- **Sometimes it's easy for a person born into luxury to become complacent and thus miss out on the simple things in life.**

- When was the last time you sat back and enjoyed nature—clouds, stars, butterflies, squirrels, and so on?

- **YOUTUBE SPEECH: "I AM AFRICAN" BY THABO MBEKI**

- How did Africans let Africa become what it is today?

- If Africa is the richest continent in terms of natural resources, why is it so poor?

- ## DOCUMENTARY: BLOOD DIAMONDS (2006)

- Your life has come full circle when you have evolved from being a student to becoming a teacher and then a mentor.

- Take an etiquette class.

- **Rest assured African American women: Louis Farrakhan will probably never marry a Caucasian woman.**

- Some of the most beautiful women in the world are also some of the loneliest because most men assume they are taken.

- ## NEWSFLASH: THERE'S A NEW CROP OF WOMEN WHO DON'T MIND IF THEIR HUSBANDS STRAY AS LONG

AS IT'S DONE RESPECTFULLY.

- One day soon the United States will legalize ganja smoking once the government figures out how to tax it.

- If a man offers you his seat, do him the honor of taking it.

- **NEW YORKERS: AT ALL TIMES, GIVE YOUR SEAT TO A PREGNANT WOMAN EVEN IF THERE'S EVIDENCE SHE'S RED SOX FAN.**

- Just because women have fought for and received equal rights in certain areas of society doesn't mean it's OK to let her stand while traveling on public transportation while preggers.

- **Financially support the veterans of your country.**

- Check out charities or businesses via the Better Business Bureau (BBB).

- ❖ **Human rights are gay rights.**

  - ❖ The gay rights movement is inspired by the civil rights movement.

- ❖ **DOCUMENTARY: INSIDE JOB (2010)**

- ❖ **Douche bags get things done.**

  - ❖ Everyone needs a douche bag in his or her life.

  - ❖ Violence in the human heart and mind needs a release, and it's better in movies than in real life.

- ❖ **LOVERS ROCK: BERES HAMMOND, FREDDIE MCGREGOR, GREGORY ISAACS, KEN BOOTHE, JOHN HOLT, AND DENNIS BROWN**

  - ❖ When will dictators learn?

- If you are disloyal to your citizens, why should they be loyal to you?

- **Your citizens are your number one asset; treat them as such.**

- The greed allowed to fester in some government agencies is disgusting.

- **Support the economies of developing countries; they need it and they treat you like royalty.**

- Be adventurous when it comes to food.

- If you are gay, don't marry someone of the opposite sex only to cheat on him or her with someone of the same sex.

- **ART: "THE CARD PLAYERS" BY PAUL CÉZANNE**

- Michael Jackson and Whitney Houston should be remembered for their musical contributions and not their personal lives.

- ❖ **Overconsumption of prescription pills can kill you.**

- ❖ Overconsumption in general can be debilitating.

- ❖ **Mixing prescription pills with alcohol is a lethal cocktail.**

- ❖ If you keep screwing around and acting recklessly, the grim reaper is waiting to snatch life from you.

- ❖ **If it should be administered in a hospital, it shouldn't be in your house.**

- ❖ For most immigrants, it's better to be in the projects of the United States than their birth countries.

- ❖ **Not all immigrants are like Tony Montana.**

- ❖ Immigrants are in your country because they want a better life for themselves and their families back home.

- Not every immigrant wants to live in the United States; some simply have no choice.

- **The opportunities in the US are limitless, especially when you have a valid social security number.**

- **Opportunities arise for both non-immigrants and immigrants, so you shouldn't look down on anyone because you never know what the future holds.**

- Every day is Black History Month.

- The streets of the US are not paved with gold.

- **If you don't know how to use Twitter, refrain from uploading seminude pictures of yourself.**

- When traveling to a foreign country, by all means, obey the laws of that country.

- He call you—sure! You call him—maybe!

- **If you live in a house, make sure your address is clearly displayed in front so if ever you need an ambulance, the paramedics are not wasting time trying to locate your house.**

- There's way too much trash on television.

- Every woman has a little Bridget Jones in her.

- **There's nothing wrong with having a male-only facility (not strip club), as some men need a place to get away from their nagging spouses. However, it should be open to men of all races as all races can suffer**

- **from the nagging spouse syndrome.**

- **The only cure for political corruption is transparency.**

- The most powerful force in politics is the knowledgeable enfranchised voter.

- **Some celebrities knowingly make incendiary comments for publicity.**

- The impetus for some men becoming millionaires is the women who rejected them for not being attractive or rich enough.

- **Capitalism is built on an opportunistic mind-frame.**

- It doesn't matter whom you vote for as long as you vote.

- Lust sells.

- ❖ **You can always tell the wives who respect themselves, their husbands, and their children by the way they carry themselves.**

- ❖ You can always tell the husbands who respect themselves, their wives, and their children by the way they carry themselves.

- ❖ **When buying a gift for someone, buy something *that person* would like instead of getting something *you* would like.**

- ❖ Forget diamonds; real estate is a girl's best friend.

- ❖ The road to becoming president is definitely paved with good intentions.

- ❖ **The title marriage should be reserved for two people who when they have unprotected**

sex have the potential to procreate.

- There's nothing wrong with civil unions.

- Gay people should be allowed to serve openly in the military.

- **According to Dr. Gary Chapman, the five love languages are: quality time, words of affirmation, acts of service, receiving gifts, and physical touch.**

- If your girlfriend or boyfriend cheated on you with multiple men or women, there is no need to disclose that information on Twitter.

- **Social media isn't the place to air an ex-lover's dirty laundry.**

- Some conspiracies are only in your mind.

- **It's morally reprehensible for some Western companies to use citizens of Third-World countries as guinea pigs.**

- Are some Westerners forgetting the *Christ* in Christmas?

- **It's unfortunate that children are more aware of Santa Claus than of God.**

- To be extraordinary, you must think outside the box.

- **PEOPLE: STEVE JOBS**

- **The sexualization of children in pop culture is appalling.**

- **What's up with giving posthumous awards? Hopefully, Leonardo DiCaprio will win an**

Academy Award while he's alive.

❖ Is marijuana healthier that tobacco? If so, why is it illegal?

❖ **What has President Barack Obama done for African Americans? He became President of the United States.**

❖ Some of the issues this generation is fighting to accomplish might not be realized in our lifetime.

❖ **It's disheartening that every time a school needs to be built, a child is in need, or a family is destitute, the name that springs to mind is Oprah Winfrey. We all need to do our part; there are others more financially capable than her (check out 2012 *Forbes* list of the richest people).**

- Unfortunately in 2012, being Caucasian and gay in certain parts of the United States is still better than being African American.

- **The rest of the world is very aware of how some African Americans are treated by their peers in their own country.**

- In some circles, when African Americans are abroad representing United States, they are deemed American, but when they return to their homeland, they are treated like second class citizens, why is that?

- **AFRICAN AMERICANS: NOT ALL CAUCASIAN PEOPLE ARE THE SAME—SOME CAN ACTUALLY BE TRUSTED AND ARE IN YOUR BEST INTEREST.**

- Don't disregard a person based on his or her ancestors.

- **Some Caucasians might have instituted slavery in the United States but**

> **there were also some who fought tirelessly—and even died trying—to abolish it.**

- There's so much diversity prominent in certain states in the United States, but this isn't represented in television commercials. Why is that?

- **Some celebrities can be as fat as they want to be as long as they are healthy and keep churning out good work.**

- Contemporary tokenism is very subtle.

- What's up with husbands taking their wives last name?

- **Women who post semi-nude pictures of themselves on social media are either desperate for attention, or have too much time on their hands.**

CHAPTER 9

LIFE

***
Introduction

Why was I born?

For a good portion of my life I've been contemplating this question.

I'm not the partying type, I love being at home, and while I'm locked up in my room, I often times find myself examining this question over and over again.

Why did my mother carry me full term and not abort me as so many other children have been?

Why have I experienced all I have so far?

Why is my life easier/harder than some?

Why was I born in Jamaica, West Indies?

Why did my mother move to the United Stated and drag me along?

Why wasn't I 16 & Pregnant? Actually, this one is easy to answer; my mother would have *killed* me.

These *why* questions are the stories of my life.

I first got introduced to the word *why* when I was about four or five, and my mother drilled it into my head that whenever someone asked me a question, I should always ask him or her why, no matter who he or she was. She would live to regret this as there were many times when she was thoroughly miffed that I would ask her why when she asked me to do something.

For instance:

Mom: McKenzie, can you please go and wash the dishes?

Me: Why? Why don't you do it or why don't you ask Racquel or Andrew to do it? Why are you always asking me to do stuff? Don't you see I'm busy pondering why was I born to parents who can't afford to have a nanny to wash the dishes?

Needless to say, these situations didn't turn out well for me, especially since I had a no-nonsense Caribbean mother.

In the decades I've spent examining all the why questions and so much more, I've come to a conclusion. Everything in life happens for a reason, and nothing in life is coincidental. It is all part of a master plan whose blueprint was created long before I was a dream in my mother's soul.

There are few things I believe in life, and one of them is I was meant to be here. I was meant to be born; I was meant to have the parents I have; I was meant to have the childhood I had; I was meant experience all I did in my teenage years; I was meant to experience all I did in my career; I was meant experience the abandonment of a parent; I was meant to write this book. I was meant to have this life; it was all meant for me, and for the first time in my life, I *own* it.

We were all born for a purpose and I know sometimes it's

hard to concentrate on finding out what that purpose is because we're distracted by folly, but if we don't search for the purpose of our birth we will never find it.

LIFE

* * *

- ❖ Is your life...lifeless or priceless?

- ❖ **If you were to die today, would have any regrets?**

- ❖ At this stage in your life, are you honestly happy? If not, what are you doing about that fact?

- ❖ Today can be the beginning of the rest of your life.

- ❖ **Life begins when you decide to begin living it.**

- ❖ Plan to leave this world a better place.

- ❖ The world should be a better place because of your existence.

- ❖ **You have the potential to influence the world either in a good or bad way. Make the right choice!**

- ❖ There are always choices in life; learn to make the right ones.

- ❖ **There will be times in life where you will have to bite your tongue and swallow the blood; in other words, there will be times when you will have to keep your mouth shut to move forward.**

- ❖ Indecision is a decisive decision.

- ❖ You are responsible for the results of your indecision.

- ❖ **Activities that make us feel good today may turn out to be detrimental to us tomorrow.**

- ❖ Instead of lamenting over the circumstances in your life, accept and make the best of them.

- ❖ Use the discontentment in your life to make your situation better.

- ❖ **If you don't search for the meaning of life, you will never find it.**

- Your life is your story.

- Looking for a cause to pursue? Dissect your life.

- **Live life in a meaningful way.**

- Life should be taken seriously, but find time to enjoy it.

- Living is different from existing; do you know the difference?

- **Most folks just exist—you should plan to live.**

- If the thrill of living is gone, it's your responsibility to get it back.

- Life is in seconds and phases.

- In the blink of an eye, your life could be over, so appreciate every second of it.

- **There's strength in exhibiting your weaknesses.**

- It's unwise to let anyone exploit you based on your weaknesses.

- It's easier for some people to point out your faults than it is for them to recognize their own.

- Loving someone is a choice.

- **If you are going to love someone, you have to love the good, the bad, and the ugly part of him or her.**

- Chaos breeds insanity.

- Instead of waiting or assuming that the next person is making an impact, why don't *you* do something?

- It's reckless to assume; make sure.

- **The only person you can be 100 percent sure of is yourself.**

- Give good love even if it's not initially reciprocated.

- Wealth can be deceiving and blinding.

- ❖ **Money can't buy you sanity, but it sure can make you insane.**

- ❖ People keep hate alive.

- ❖ Purity of the mind is possible.

- ❖ **The greatest moment of your life will be unplanned.**

- ❖ Live for your one moment in time.

- ❖ Learn to find other ways to celebrate your successes without consistently buying yourself stuff you can't afford.

- ❖ **The difference between a memorable life and mediocre death is the fighter in you.**

- ❖ All children should be celebrated.

- ❖ **There are four types of people: dreamers,**

talkers, doers, and watchers.

❖ Some people are talkers; others are doers. Which one are you?

❖ Getting older is very sobering.

❖ Try not to wander through life aimlessly.

❖ Watching your life slip away from you is very sobering.

❖ Dead people are deaf, so if you have something to say, say it before the people you love die.

❖ It sucks when your loved ones are conspiring against you.

❖ Some years will be good and others not so swell.

❖ The years between your birth and death are what matters most.

❖ The day of your death should be far more

important than the day of your birth.

❖ Life is short, and the years are flying by.

❖ To live an abundant life, you don't need lots of money.

❖ **To be rich in spirit is worth its weight in gold.**

❖ There are many ways to get the same result.

❖ Not everyone is like you, but that is the beauty of life.

❖ **One of the reasons there's so much devastation in the world is because most people are selfish instead of selfless.**

❖ Caring without action is ineffective.

❖ **Common sense is based on your background; therefore, at some point**

in your life, you may have lacked it.

❖ In your lifetime, you are bl5ssed if you have at least three trustworthy friends.

❖ **Never return to the same drink you just walked away from while in a bar/club.**

❖ If you can't hold your liquor, take necessary precautions.

❖ You can't make someone want better for him or herself.

❖ **Accept the fact that you will have to learn to stay out of your own way.**

❖ A person is free to judge you, and you are free to ignore his or her judgment.

❖ To have successful relationships, you have to meet people where they are.

❖ **Not everyone you meet is at your spiritual or**

intellectual level, and that is OK.

❖ Instead of leaving footprints in the sand, leave them on the hearts of the people you meet.

❖ It is your life, but it's not entirely about you.

❖ **There are three types of decisions: bad, good, and excellent.**

❖ **As you get older, you should be making more good and excellent decisions.**

❖ Experience gives you the upper hand.

❖ Every little bit counts.

❖ **Your life is complicated enough without you consistently sabotaging yourself.**

- ❖ It's OK if people judge you because when all is said and done, their judgments are irrelevant; they just have not received the memo yet.

- ❖ **Wherever you go, you take your convictions with you.**

- ❖ Always let someone know your location.

- ❖ No man is an island; you need people.

- ❖ Two is better than one; there is power in numbers.

- ❖ **It's easier to catch bees with honey than with vinegar.**

- ❖ Every day you are able to open your eyes is a day to be grateful for.

- ❖ **When you are young, you put things off until tomorrow. However, as you get older, you realize today *is* tomorrow.**

- It's imprudent to be a Band-Aid person; attack a problem from its root.

- You can let life beat you, or you can whip its tush.

- **There's no need to put yourself in debt burying a dead person.**

- You are wanted and not needed for Godly assignments.

- **If you are not up for the assignment, God will find someone else.**

- Preparation is the key to living a successful life.

- Having the right perspective is important because it will determine the trajectory of your life.

- **It's reckless to let the actions or inactions of others determine the trajectory of your life.**

- No one owes you anything, so when you do favors for people, don't expect anything in return.

- People don't consistently do favors for free; eventually they are going to ask for a favor in return, which might be the beginning of you becoming their mule.

- **All you have to do is pay your taxes and die, nothing else is obligatory.**

- There should be nothing material you need.

- **The only merchandise you deserve is that for which you can afford to pay cash.**

- Be appreciative of the little things in life.

- Even if your parents failed you, you don't have to fail yourself.

- **At some point in your adult life, you have to let bygones be bygones and stop blaming your parents for your current state of affairs.**

- It's risky to depend on your electronic devices for everything.

- Don't let life pass you by like a train through a station.

- **The biggest differences between children and adults are children's incredible abilities to be faithful and to forgive and forget.**

- Loving yourself is like the progress bar on your favorite website; it will take time to achieve.

- Have a serving heart, and serve with glee.

- **Sometimes it's good to do things you don't feel like doing simply to challenge yourself.**

- You are a work in progress that isn't completed until death.

- **Death is final, so do what you can to live as long as you can.**

- Tell and show people how much they mean to you before they are on their deathbeds.

- You are not God, so stop acting like it.

- **Lack of preparation on your part doesn't mean diddlysquat to a prepared person.**

- If you want to destroy your life, fine, but don't take innocent lives with you.

- **No human being is innocent; we are all guilty of something.**

- Disappointments are the seasonings of life.

- If your life is perfect, it must be boring.

- There's nothing you can't overcome or achieve.

- **You may be down, but don't count yourself out until you draw your last breath.**

- A little positivity goes a long way.

- **Find out the facts instead of jumping to conclusions.**

- Learn to make informed decisions on your own.

- **If you ask what's perceived as a silly question, don't be surprised when you get a silly answer.**

- Stop mentally torturing yourself worrying about what people think.

- **One of the most important questions to ask is why.**

- Perseverance is underrated.

- If you try hard enough, you can talk yourself into anything.

- **If you try hard enough, you can talk yourself out**

of anything, especially your destiny.

- If you try hard enough, you can justify any bad action.

- Stop talking to yourself and start talking to God.

- **If the last three generations of your family have been living in low-income housing, be the one to break the cycle.**

- Keep away from the gossipmonger at church, work, gym, and so on.

- Be a cheerful giver, and give without remorse.

- **Respect everyone's religious beliefs.**

- It's unbeneficial to force your religion on anyone, as you would not want someone to do that to you.

- **Whether you agree or not, you still have to**

respect someone's decision.

❖ Stop trying to impose your lifestyle on others. Learn from the past, but at the same time don't let it consume your present.

❖ **The past you can tell but can't change, and the future you can't tell but can change.**

❖ Learn to pick sense out of nonsense.

❖ **Not all advice is trustworthy or deserves consideration.**

❖ Lack of consideration can get you killed.

❖ Leaving your house daily is an act of faith.

❖ **Discover yourself before you discover someone else.**

❖ Don't be afraid of yourself.

- ❖ **Almost everyone compromises when there is something in it for him or herself.**

- ❖ It's reckless to put your life on hold for someone, and you shouldn't ask anyone to do that for you.

- ❖ **Spend time praying, as this is effective and a good release.**

- ❖ Fast for clarity or to save money on meals.

- ❖ **With a grateful heart, you can make the best of any situation.**

- ❖ For some, failure is simply not an option.

- ❖ **A person's life should be valued immeasurably.**

- ❖ Guard your mouth to keep yourself out of trouble.

- ❖ When in doubt, keep your mouth shut.

- ❖ **To save your life, sometimes it's best to keep your mouth shut while in precarious situations.**

- ❖ To live to fight another day, sometimes it's best to run away from a fight.

- ❖ **A foolish person never met a fight he or she didn't want to participate in.**

- ❖ Only fools love to argue.

- ❖ Keep it short and sweet (KISS).

- ❖ No one is expected to know everything, so don't act like it.

- ❖ **If you don't know, ask instead of guessing.**

- ❖ As you get older, you should be more interested in the facts than the details.

- ❖ **Celebrate the people in your life.**

- ❖ **Wisdom is attainable, but you will have to go looking for it.**

- ❖ Seeking revenge is futile and only depletes your soul.

- ❖ Some people truly don't know any better.

- ❖ **Accept people for who they are instead of trying to make them into something they are not.**

- ❖ Being a people pleaser is exhausting.

- ❖ **As you get older, you should become a more peaceful and contented person.**

- ❖ Try something new at least once a month.

- ❖ **Running away is never the answer.**

- **You can never run from yourself.**

- Right is right and wrong will get you off track.

- It can take you years to recover from making bad decisions.

- **Unfortunately, bad things happen to good people, and good things happen to bad people—that's just the way life is.**

- There's some good in every person.

- **Instead of judging, try to understand.**

- You were born with everything you need to succeed in life.

- Laziness leads to poverty.

- **A person of integrity walks confidently and sleeps soundly.**

- **Integrity is both who you are and what you do—you can't separate them.**

  - Integrity is both who you are and what you do behind closed doors.

- **It's to your benefit to avoid strife.**

- **Bad company can indeed corrupt good character.**

  - Some people inadvertently bring danger home with them in the form of the company they keep.

  - Be careful not to allow yourself to be used or abused.

- **Sometimes it's best to keep your innermost thoughts to yourself.**

  - Where there's smoke, there's usually a fire.

- **Life is not a game, so don't play with it.**

- If you don't hate your character, you will never strive to change it.

- **There is a time and a season for everything.**

- Think of life in terms of levels—you will not get to level two unless you pass level one.

- **It's unwise to succumb to blackmail, because your blackmailer will always be back for more.**

- When times are good be happy; when times are bad be happy.

- **FACT OF LIFE: GOOD PEOPLE DIE YOUNG, AND BAD PEOPLE LIVE LONG.**

- A smile brightens your face and keeps it youthful.

- **If you don't ask, you will not receive.**

- Even if you don't go looking for trouble, it might still find you.

- People shouldn't be confused with animals.

- **It's understandable if you love animals more than people, but loving difficult people makes you a better person.**

- Treat people better than animals.

- Travel to see how the rest of the world lives; you will be glad you did.

- **Having supporters is great, but learn to be your own #1 supporter.**

- At some point, you will have to stop blaming yourself for past failures.

- **Instead of asking yourself, why me, ask yourself, why *not* me.**

- **You are amazingly beautiful; you just have not discovered it yet.**

- Never feel guilty for doing the right thing.

- **Learn to inspire others.**

- No one can believe in you the way you can.

- **One more time will suck you right back in.**

- Silence is golden most of the time.

- Your actions always speak louder than your words.

- **You have to be in it to win it.**

- Surround yourself with people who are wiser than you are and who bring out the best in you.

- One *little* idea can yield substantial results.

- **Always offer the same grace you would like in return.**

- **You have so much untapped potential it's unbelievable.**

- There's a lot of potential sleeping in you; when will you awaken it?

- **Far too many people negate the importance of simply showing up.**

- You have not lived until you have *thought* of killing yourself.

- **It's imprudent to let debt collectors or collection agencies bring you to the brink of suicide.**

- **Committing suicide is selfish because whether you know it or not, there is someone who is going**

to be profoundly impacted by your absence.

❖ Letting yourself get distracted by small things will only prevent you from reaching for bigger things.

❖ **Life isn't fair, but it hasn't always been unfair to you either.**

❖ Waiting in anticipation is nerve racking but the joy of finally getting what you want is thrilling.

❖ Everyone needs somewhere to call home.

❖ **There will be times in your life where you'll have to bite your tongue and swallow the blood.**

❖ If you don't have anything productive to say about someone, don't say anything at all.

❖ **If you can't say something positive about someone, don't**

add fuel to the fire by saying something negative.

- Dancing in the rain can be invigorating.

- Nothing is wrong with considering rainy days as Michael Buble days.

- **Keep your negativity and misery contained.**

- No one likes being in the company of a miserable person.

- A positive attitude will add years to your life.

- There's always a positive in every negative situation; you just have to search for it.

- **The people most likely to tell you the truth are the ones who want nothing from you.**

- You are perfect just the way you are, but there's always room for improvement.

- The race isn't for the swift but for the person who is faithful enough to persevere.

- **Not everything you see is as it appears.**

- Free yourself from mental slavery, or you will torture yourself to death.

- **Only you can free yourself from mental slavery.**

- You are the reason you can't move forward.

- **It's not your needs that get you in trouble or credit card debt, but your wants.**

- You shouldn't want everything you see.

- There's a big difference between needs and wants.

- **You really don't need material items to make you happy.**

- No material item in the world will make you happy.

- Your happiness shouldn't be contingent on how much stuff you have.

- **Never be jealous of your neighbors for what they have because you don't know how they got it, and you don't know if it makes them happy.**

- Most people don't know the true meaning of happiness.

- **You should always think the best of people, but don't overlook the reality of their behavior.**

- To the best of your ability, try to live in harmony with people, knowing that not everyone knows what harmony means.

- Learn to be content with yourself.

- **Inaction on your part is still action.**

- War is never the answer.

- **No matter the outcome, no one ever wins in a war.**

- Torture might get you an answer but not necessarily the right one.

- **DOCUMENTARY: <u>THE FOG OF WAR: ELEVEN LESSONS FROM THE LIFE OF ROBERT S. MCNAMARA</u> (2003)**

- It's not the job of the US to liberate the world.

- **Regardless of race, color, creed, and sexuality, we all have red blood flowing through our veins.**

- One person can change the world for better or worse, and it could be you.

- **You are a tiny fragment of a tremendous puzzle, but your piece is still very important.**

  - In life, we all have different roles to play, and your role is very important no matter how small it might seem.

  - Never let anyone tell you or make you feel as if you are not needed or wanted.

- **You are only entitled to respect and civility.**

  - There's no such thing as a coincidence; everything happens for a reason.

- **Your life is what you make it.**

  - If you hate your life, work on changing it day by day, little by little.

  - Stop blaming others for your bad decisions.

- **Don't be bitter becluse you let someone control**

your life, and it hasn't turned out well.

- This is your time; this is your moment. Let no one take that away from you.

- Be passionate about your life and future.

- **Embracing what is good for you is never easy but is so worth it.**

- Balance is extremely important for a healthy and stable life.

- Be careful to whom you entrust your mind.

- **READ: "THE PURPOSE DRIVEN LIFE" BY RICK WARREN**

- Live purposefully.

- **Drifting through life is a waste of a life.**

- Your life is forgettable unless you make it unforgettable.

- **Every person has his or her own private hell that he or she is trying to live through.**

- You will not get along with everyone, but do your best to get along with someone.

- **Death exists to teach you how to appreciate life and love people.**

- Be as transparent as possible about your struggles.

- **Be generous with your time and resources.**

- It's reckless to make promises you can't keep or have no intention of ever fulfilling.

- Think before you make a promise to a child.

- **You have to choose to move on from a bad situation.**

- What is for you is for you—you only have to claim it.

- **The only way a person can ruin your life is if you let him or her.**

- Don't let your desire for power cloud your judgment.

- **Your need to be better than the next person leads to your lack of civility.**

- Whatever is done in the dark will eventually become known; it's only a matter of time.

- Love your life because it could be so much worse.

- **Your thoughts are your worst enemy.**

- Your mind dictates your actions.

- If you don't know who you are, how can you strive to be a better person?

- **Don't rent who you are; own it!**

- There's a difference between being satisfied and contented. Which one are you?

- **Be a rebel with a cause.**

- Daydreaming about how to escape your reality? What is the plan?

- **Laugh aloud most of the time, but not with food in your mouth.**

- Sometimes it is good to sit back and enjoy the show.

- **Occasionally, let someone take care of you for a change.**

- Never give up your independence to become dependent on someone else.

- **Live your life with your death in mind.**

- Allow the people in your life to tell you the truth without fear of retaliation or rejection.

- There's a huge difference between being respected and being feared.

❖ Document and share your journey.

- Know enough about life to know that you don't know much.

- Real beauty flows and glows from within.

❖ Your life should be filled with adventure.

- Be a student of life.

❖ Learn to accept constructive criticism.

- Don't ask for someone's opinion and then be offended when it's not what you expected.

❖ A wise person takes advantage of God's gifts.

- Having expectations can distort the value of an experience.

- What is for you is for you as long as you go along with the plan.

- **Pay more attention to your reactions than to other people's actions.**

- It's not what you wear on the outside; it's how you feel on the inside.

- **Don't let the negativity of life permeate your soul.**

- To have joy in your life is delightful.

- **It's better to live without material goods than to have them and be miserable.**

- People will exploit your desperation.

- **Analyze situations on a case-by-case basis.**

- People generally support you because they like you.

- ❖ **Insecurity is revealed when words are plentiful.**

- ❖ Where there's life, there's sure to be death.

- ❖ Be mindful of the way you talk to peo16le.

- ❖ **Life isn't supposed to be easy, but it also isn't supposed to be difficult.**

- ❖ Eat, drink, pray, and have good laughs with friends.

- ❖ There's a huge difference between listening and hearing.

- ❖ **To experience life to the fullest, you need a heart of understanding.**

- ❖ Death makes life possible.

- ❖ Because some people have never been loved, all they want to do is destroy.

- ❖ Every person wants to belong and feel part of a team.

- Some people waste their time dissecting the small things; hence, they can't see the bigger picture.

- **Money as a tangible can't replace love that is an intangible.**

- **Hits, misses, victories, disappointments, love, rejection, contentment, discontentment, sadne19s, and happiness make life unpredictable and worth living.**

- Max out your life and not your credit card.

- **Instead of always buying stuff, let necessity be the mother of your inventions.**

- Unfortunately, the majority of people don't care about social issues unless someone close to them is affected.

- Unfortunately, to get a person's attention, the situation must affect him or her directly.

- **Happiness is based on your state of mind.**

- Instead of waiting for help, how about learning to help yourself?

- The time you spend waiting for help, you could have MacGyvered yourself out of that situation.

- **To meet your hero, simply look in the mirror.**

- Refrain from saying anything you might have to apologize for later.

- **Loving yourself isn't only empowering, but also one of the best things you can do for yourself.**

- There are three things that should never be late: direct deposits, child-support checks, and periods.

- Some people think they are invincible until they stop breathing.

- **Most people don't realize death is simply a heartbeat away.**

- In order for your relationships to be prosperous, you have to let go of your ego.

- **It's reckless to let anyone convince you to stay in mediocrity.**

- Persevere, persevere, and keep on persevering.

- **As you get older, you should become better instead of bitter.**

- The most successful people are bold.

- **Learn to enjoy your journey on the way to your destination.**

- If you want something, you have to go after it.

❖ **There's nothing in the world more eye opening than being young and naive.**

❖ Wisdom and discernment can be contagious if you primarily associate with people who are wise and discerning.

❖ Anyone can teach you something about life, so be open.

❖ **Find contentment and peace in knowing there's something only you can do in a specific way and that should make you feel like one in a gazillion.**

❖ Some people are oblivious to the way their actions or inactions affect you; it's your responsibility to let them know.

❖ Some people are unfortunately oblivious to the world they live in.

- ❖ **Your success primarily depends on you and you alone.**

- ❖ Some people should be seen and not heard.

- ❖ **Being a fighter helps you be stronger and wiser; however, pick your battles wisely.**

- ❖ The show *must* go on with or without you, but it will be so much better with you in it.

- ❖ **Learn to fight your own battles; it makes you stronger.**

- ❖ At some point in your life, you will have to pay the piper.

- ❖ If you know you are a procrastinator, always create do-it day deadlines.

- ❖ **Never lose your yearning for learning.**

- ❖ When you stop learning, you start dying.

- **An educated person isn't necessarily a smart person and an uneducated person isn't necessarily a stupid person.**

- Some people are book smart, and some people are street smart; appreciate them both.

- **It's beneficial to be both street smart and book smart.**

- There's value in being street smart.

- **Some doors should never be opened at all.**

- If you make a bad decision, admit to it and move on.

- **Don't be so quick to discredit someone for making a mistake; instead, give him or her an opportunity to fix it.**

- Learn to believe in second chances.

- **Change takes time, patience, and opportunity.**

- Forgiveness is a work in progress.

- Avoid stereotypes and stereotypical behavior.

- **There's a monumental difference between self-preservation and selfishness.**

- Occasionally, you will have to pray, God give me strength and grant me peace during these troubling times.

- **At some point, you have to realize that you are too old to be making the same mistakes you made ten or fifteen years ago.**

- Only God can execute justice but fairness is humanly possible.

- ❖ **Create social programs that benefit both boys and girls.**

- ❖ Exceptionally good liars are not afraid to look you in the eyes.

- ❖ **Look the part, talk the part, and most importantly be the part.**

- ❖ Some people are in so much pain, they are completely numb. Are you one of these people?

- ❖ **Some people build you up so they can tear you down.**

- ❖ Your pen is a mighty tool; use it more often.

- ❖ Nothing is written in stone; there are exceptions to every rule.

- ❖ **F.E.A.R. = Forging earnestly ahead with resolve.**

- ❖ The time is never right to face your fears.

- **Fear can be immobilizing, unless you decide to keep on moving no matter what.**

- The things you are afraid of doing are the things you *must* do.

- It is good to receive but even better to give.

- **As a Christian, your job is to carry to the good news to nonbelievers with the understanding that you can't force anyone to accept it.**

- Believe what you believe, and respect what others believe.

- **You should spend more time working out *your* salvation with fear and trembling rather than being consumed with what the next Christian is doing.**

- The devil uses your life to testify against you.

- Evil is very patient.

- It's human to feel but think before you act on those feelings.

- **Some Christians with psychological problems need more than prayer; they need professional help.**

- Sticks and stones may break your bones but an abusive tongue is even more destructive.

- Perseverance builds and enhances character.

- **There's beauty in your imperfection.**

- If you don't hope for a better day, it will never come.

- **Hope only comes to the hopeful.**

- Life is about vision, hope, faith, execution, perseverance, humility, and most importantly love.

- **For doing what you feel is morally correct, you may be considered persona non grata in certain social circles; that is fine because as least you get a good night's sleep.**

- Haste definitely makes waste; it's better to take your time to do something right than rush and do it wrong.

- To know better isn't necessarily to do better.

- **Some people are only around you to seduce you, and as soon as they get what they want they will discard you.**

- You should make a bucket list every month.

- **Your truth is your truth and you shouldn't let anyone take that away from you.**

- The truth is the truth and will never become untrue no matter how many times it's reiterated.

- The only way to get to the truth is by listening and learning to ask the right questions.

- **One of the benefits of life is that you get an opportunity to learn how to figure things out for yourself.**

- Anyone can fail at life but anyone can also succeed; it's about frame of mind.

- Some people have an easy life while others have a difficult life, but at least they all get a chance to experience life.

- Strategies and tactics are essential in both business and life.

- **If a person is doing a life sentence in Sing Sing, it's dumb to allow him or her to manipulate you into doing his or her dirty work on the outside.**

- ❖ **Deep-rooted arrogance can keep you closed off from beneficial opportunities.**

- ❖ We all need friends as life wouldn't be the same without people to laugh and talk with.

- ❖ Some people are already on edge; do your best to not push them over.

- ❖ **No government agency or representative is universally infallible but they should be held accountable for the decisions they make.**

- ❖ It's naïve for any citizen to think that his or her government is 100 percent honest or transparent; that's not feasible.

- ❖ **Corrupt people will exploit your deep-rooted hatred and bitterness.**

- Who says you can't be an optimist and a realist?

- Some people who consistently make "I am" statements do it to convince themselves of something they aspire to but are not confident they are.

- Humans can't make other humans happy.

- **Don't depend on others to make you happy, if you are depressed, figure out the source of your depression and take steps to counteract it.**

- Have no interactions with the nemesis of someone you love.

- **Regardless of the outcome, there's freedom, peace, and contentment in doing the right thing and telling the truth.**

- Deceit + Deceit = More Deceit

❖ Learn to accept compliments and encouragement.

- ❖ It's a major turn off when someone compliments you and you respond negatively.
  For instance:
  Me: Great job on your presentation
  You: Really, I thought I sucked; I made so many mistakes….

❖ Don't fool yourself, most of your adult issues stem from unresolved childhood issues.

- ❖ The sooner you accept the circumstances surrounding your life, the happier you will be.

- ❖ Most destructive human behaviors are learned, if you learned to do it, you can also learn to undo it.

- ❖ Where you are today is where you are supposed to be, however, tomorrow doesn't have to be today.

❖ Your life is your testimony.

CHAPTER 10

SPIRITUALITY

* * *

Introduction

I first got introduced to God via my parents through church. At that time, going to church was like going to the school; it lasted from 9:00 a.m. until 3:00 p.m.

It takes children quite a few years to grasp the concept of God; hence, I believe he loves children and puts up with adults.

I was also taught about God in school via my Christian Family Life (CFL) class, and there were many spirited conversations, which in hindsight I reveled in. One particular discussion was whether God the father, the Son, and the Holy Spirit were one entity.

There were times in my childhood when I prayed feverishly, whether it was to calm the storm that was developing at home or to ask for better grades. I didn't know if God heard me; nonetheless, I prayed. I had no understanding of God and treated him like he was a genie in bottle. Even so, God was a constant in my life.

While I was growing up, my dad was the apple of my eye; I revered him, and I thought he could do no wrong and conquer and slay all dragons. In between my mother moving to the United States when I was nine and puberty, my relationship with my dad became strained and at times very toxic and unhealthy.

He made the decision to send me and my sister to live with

my mother abruptly. I didn't want to go because even though I had come to resent my dad, I still thought he needed someone to take care of him if he got sick. I remember verbalizing my feelings and my dad saying that if my sister went so would I.

At that time, I thought this was the ultimate betrayal from a person I had loved so much and was so dedicated to. In hindsight, I think that was one of the best decisions he could have made as a responsible parent.

Through all this turmoil, God remained the only constant entity in my life. He has never changed; he has always been there and loved me through the good times and the bad.

Make no mistake, I know who I am, and I know there are times when I'm deceitful, mean-spirited, wretched, annoying, judgmental, and sanctimonious, but he has never turned his face away from me even when I was head deep in debauchery.

Whether you choose to acknowledge it or not, you are a spiritual being. You come from a royal bloodline, and I'm not talking about the British royal family.

Recently, a survey reported that fewer and fewer people believe in God, and given the current state of the world and how Christians—including myself—fail to present God as we should, I can certainly understand; however, in order for you to live the life you are were destined to live you have to get on the same page as God.

I've been part of organized religion for years, and I've seen many things, some good or not so good, but through it all I've persevered. There are some things I struggle immensely with, but I'm confident that in due time my heart will be open and receptive to healing.

God isn't a high-profile person where in order for you to get to him, you have to call his agent or business manager. God is right there next to you, right now. All you have to do is start talking and get yourself a Bible.

Like any other relationship, you have to prepare yourself, as you won't get everything you want when you want it. There will be times of discipline; there will be times of sorrow; and there will be times of laughter, but it all happens to refine your character.

I've seen and experienced it, where people have let other people cajole them into thinking that in order for them to access God, they need to go through them; that's malarkey, but you will only know this if you read the bible for yourself.

I've observed that most people do what they want when they want and if something is a priority for them, they go to great lengths to make it happen.

Therefore, if a person wants a relationship with God he or she will seek it just like the woman who wants to marry a basketball player or the man who wants to become a senior vice president of a Fortune 500 company by the time he is thirty-five.

When all is said and done, we have a choice in how our lives turn out. Some of the following anecdotes, I really wish someone had imparted to me when I was younger; I wouldn't have taken them all to heart because I'm stubborn like that, but I definitely would have benefited from some of them.

* * *

- ❖ Whether you accept or acknowledge it, you are a spiritual being.

- ❖ **Being spiritual has different meanings to different people at different times in their lives.**

- ❖ The only constant in civilization is God.

- ❖ **God is the same yesterday, today, tomorrow, and forever.**

- ❖ Not everyone is spiritually at the same place and this is OK.

- ❖ Let God define you instead of people.

- ❖ **People are much more judgmental, ungracious, merciless, and critical than God.**

❖ MUSIC: "AMAZING GRACE" BY SUSAN BOYLE

- ❖ There's beauty in innocence.

- ❖ Nothing is pure when human beings are involved.

- ❖ **Loving yourself is divine intervention.**

- ❖ Whether you believe in God or not, he believes in you.

- ❖ God is orchestrating your every move even though you don't believe in him.

- ❖ **God is the ultimate puppet master.**

- ❖ Nothing is impossible with God on your side.

- ❖ It is wise to be mindful of the spiritual world you live in.

- ❖ **God loves you whether you love him or not.**

- ❖ When was the last time you took a good look at your spirit in the mirror?

SPIRITUALITY

- ❖ **Whether you believe in God or not, you will always be his child.**

- ❖ Always try to save a life, as it might be your own.

- ❖ Far too many people take life for granted and end up regretting it.

- ❖ Right now is it 2:52 a.m. est. on September 23, 2012; 2:53 a.m. est. on September 23, 2012, is promised to no one.

- ❖ **It doesn't matter what people think of you; all that matters is what God says about you.**

- ❖ God loves gay people.

- ❖ **You are signed, sealed, and can be delivered, according to God's plan.**

- ❖ Don't stoop to someone's level; instead, lift him or her up to yours.

- ❖ Seek the riches of life instead of financial gains.

- **Think of yourself as being like fine wine—getting better with time.**

- Life is short; maximize your moments.

- **Faithfulness is actionable, but faithlessness is actionless.**

- Church isn't a building.

- **You need your church community to help keep you focused on the prize.**

- There should be reverence in the house of God.

- No sex in the pew before Sunday service.

- When God reveals something, he wants it to be dealt with immediately.

- ❖ **Learn not to be enablers; instead, learn to disable bad situations.**

- ❖ Tell yourself consistently how awesome you are because even if you don't believe it initially, after a while, you will start believing it.

- ❖ Be a participant in your life—not a spectator.

- ❖ **How long will you continue to be a spectator before getting involved?**

- ❖ The characters change, but the circumstances of life are still the same.

- ❖ Every person needs to be processed by God.

- ❖ **It's unwise to waste your life chasing after meaningless things.**

- ❖ All people are blessed; they just don't know it.

- ❖ Never blame people for looking out for their best interests.

- **When digging a grave for someone, make sure you dig one next to it for yourself.**

- Random acts of kindness are good for your soul.

- **MUSIC: "THIS LITTLE LIGHT OF MINE" BY SAM COOKE**

- God speaks to both men and women.

- **Mean what you say and say exactly what you mean.**

- Cut the crap and be forthcoming and honest with people.

- Be glad people can't buy their way into heaven; that way, everyone has a chance.

- **It's hard to keep track of lies; therefore, it's best to be honest but in a loving way.**

- Self-sabotage is self-destructive.

SPIRITUALITY

- If you want something, ask God, but realize it might take decades to get.

- Your credibility is all you have.

- **Greed is destructive.**

- God isn't an automated teller machine (ATM).

- What you put into your relationship with God is what you will get out of it.

- **It's dumb to sleep with the leader of your church; it will not turn out well for you.**

- Respect your body as the temple it's supposed to be.

- Recognize that we live in a depraved world, and equip yourself with the necessary tools to counteract it.

- It's a Burger King world; you can have any religion your way.

- **Death is inevitable, but instead of waiting to die, live as if you were dying.**

- Who made the heavens and the earth? It was not you, so who are you to judge?

❖ God never abandons you...even if you abandon him.

- God has an all-points bulletin (APB) out on you right now.

- Learn to forgive yourself.

❖ God loves the little children and puts up with adults.

- Integrity counts for more than you know.

- Learn not to internalize other people's issues.

❖ Learn to push back when people try to dump their problems on you.

- Not everyone who claims to come in the name of the Lord should be trusted.

- Just because someone is a Christian doesn't mean he or she doesn't consistently struggle spiritually.

- **Whether he or she chooses to admit it or not, every Christian struggles with sin in one way or another.**

- There's a little voice inside; spend more time listening to it rather than ignoring it.

- **The devil thrives in darkness.**

- Being self-controlled and disciplined will help you to live a healthier life.

- Youth is wasted on the young only if they waste their youth.

- **Be proactive instead of reactive.**

- Wisdom isn't a friend to a foolish man.

- For some people, life is too hard to live; hence, they kill themselves.

- **Invest in your future by investing in God.**

- Being humble can go a long way.

- It's unbeneficial to let your pride or stubbornness get in the way of your success.

- **Success isn't measured by how much money you accumulate; it's measured by how you live your life.**

- When placed in a situation where you have to choose between being merciful and merciless, choose being merciful.

- Goodness comes back to you eventually.

- **It's ill-advised to depend on someone else to teach you about God. Go to him directly through his word.**

- You don't need to go through anyone to access God.

- Your life is richer and more fulfilling with God in it.

SPIRITUALITY

- **Squash disagreements quickly before they turn into major blowouts.**

- Don't think too highly of yourself, or you will never recognize your lowly position.

- **Apologize when you realize your actions have materialized into something toxic.**

- Matthew 5:38 says, "An eye for an eye," but what does the rest of the paragraph say?

- Loving your enemies is hard but good for your soul.

- The church isn't always a safe place.

- **NEWSFLASH: THE CHURCH IS MADE UP OF IMPERFECT PEOPLE.**

- Some Christians are spiritual bullies.

- **Just because some people can recite the**

Bible from Genesis to Revelations doesn't mean they are spiritually wise or sound.

❖ Spirituality doesn't necessarily grow with age.

❖ There are people who grow old and then there are people who just get old.

❖ It's impossible for you to grow if you keep yourself in the same environment.

❖ **You can learn something from anyone at anytime.**

❖ God created evolution.

❖ **Instead of using science to acknowledge God, some people use it to discredit him.**

❖ Don't use the creation to discredit the creator.

- **God tests the ones he love to see if they love him.**

- If you don't show up to work late, why would you show up to church late?

- Not everyone in the church is who he or she claims to be.

- **At any institution where money is donated, there will always be some level of politics involved.**

- Arrogance is a major turn-off for the growth of your spirituality.

- What sins does a baby have to repent of?

- **Priests should be allowed to marry; it's better for them to be fondling their wives than impressionable children.**

- If you believe in good and evil, then you believe in God and the devil.

- You have to believe in God in order to experience his greatness.

- **People don't consistently do favors for free; eventually they are going to ask for a favor in return, which might be the beginning of you becoming their mule.**

- To be hugged by God is like being swept up in a gust of wind.

- You will always be a child in God's eyes!

- **God isn't spiteful or vindictive.**

- God doesn't screw up the world, people do.

- **Make peace with the fact that some things will**

never be explained in your lifetime.

❖ **No one will ever be able to disprove the existence of God, not even the scientists he created.**

❖ **God created doctors, medicine, and surgery to help you when you are ill because he wants you to live as long as you can, so he can use you to fulfill his will for the world. It would be foolish to not accept their assistance.**

❖ If you are on a steady decline, don't look to drag others down with you.

❖ **Be in awe of God and not people.**

❖ God can always find a way to spin a negative situation into a positive one.

- ❖ **Wisdom will add years to your life.**

- ❖ When wisdom comes a-knocking, open the door. However, when folly comes a-knocking, slam the door shut.

- ❖ **Relying too much on your own understanding is misleading.**

- ❖ There's nothing wrong with acknowledging God.

- ❖ **No one becomes spiritually rich without making many mistakes.**

- ❖ Stop blaming God and others for your circumstances.

- ❖ **Your evil deeds will eventually ensnare you.**

- ❖ Many are your plans, but God's purpose prevails.

- ❖ God can and will break you.

❖ MUSIC: "GOD IS GOING TO CUT YOU DOWN" BY JOHNNY CASH

- ❖ God is directing your steps, and you don't even know it.

- ❖ **We are sacrificial beings.**

- ❖ This is God's show, and you are invited to participate; are you interested? Remember, your part will not remain available for too long.

- ❖ Be careful in unlocking a person's heart.

- ❖ Only God knows the hearts of men and women and their true intentions.

- ❖ **Some people fail to realize that the corruption and perversity that lives within the human heart has and will always be the same.**

- ❖ Matters of the heart are complicated.

- ❖ Pray for wisdom and understanding.

❖ The capabilities of humanity have always been known but not always realized.

- ❖ Conquer life; don't let it conquer you.

- ❖ God would love to use you to make the world a better place if you are game.

❖ God loves using imperfect people.

- ❖ At any point you can change your situation.

- ❖ As a born-again Christian, why are you so stressed?

❖ You need God more than he needs you.

- ❖ No one will ever love you as much as God does.

- ❖ God is self-sufficient; can you afford to be?

❖ Remember God in the days of your youth.

- ❖ You can only serve one master; choose wisely.

SPIRITUALITY

- Why worship someone who shares the same fate as you?

- **Sometimes God takes away the things we worship (children, jobs, cars, spouses, security, money) in order to help us stay focused on him.**

- It's useless to worry about things you can't control.

- Where there's confusion and discontent, there you will find the dark one.

- Don't let the devil have his way with you.

- **To think you are in control is an illusion.**

- If you think it's easy being a born again Christian, you are invited to try it.

- **The harvest will always be plentiful, and the workers will always be few.**

- Though seeing, most are still blind.

- Though hearing, most are still deaf.

- Sin will stifle the Holy Spirit.

- **Every person should have someone who is crazy in love with him or her no matter what.**

- If you don't atone for your wrongs, the repercussions might carry over to your children.

- **You don't have the power to prevent your comeuppance from happening.**

- Do your best and let God do the rest!

- Keep the dream between you and God until it's time for manifestation.

- Who died and made you lord of all?

- **Control your body by controlling your mind.**

- ❖ You shouldn't allow yourself to be held psychologically captive by a living or dead person.

- ❖ Abiding by the principles of the Bible isn't easy but helps you to live a healthier and happier life.

- ❖ **Just because you believe in God and do your best to live by his standards doesn't mean you will not experience hardships.**

- ❖ Meditation and prayer are very beneficial.

- ❖ **God is always listening; all you have to do is start talking.**

- ❖ Spend a couple of minutes a day just being quiet.

- ❖ Drifting from God starts little by little, day by day.

- ❖ **God forgives as long as you repent, but you will still have to live with the consequences of your actions.**

- Just because God forgives doesn't mean there will not be blowback.

- What does it mean to be spiritual and not religious?

- **If you are spiritual and not religious, you are cheating yourself out of an enriching and productive experience.**

- Stop telling people you are spiritual; it should be evident.

- Don't let the actions of others separate you from God.

- No human being can take God's place.

- **What you do beh9nd closed doors says a lot about your character.**

- The most valuable intangible you can give anyone is your time.

- **You have to prepare for life after death.**

SPIRITUALITY

- ❖ If you are God, why can't you heal yourself when you get sick?

- ❖ There's no good without bad, there's no positive without negative, there's no rich without poor, and there's no appreciation for God without being burned by the devil.

- ❖ **You are destined for greatness even if you are currently living in mediocrity.**

- ❖ All human beings—including you—are complex but there's beauty in that complexity.

- ❖ God already believes in you, when will you start believing in yourself?

- ❖ **MUSIC: "IT'S WELL WITH MY SOUL," BY JEREMY RIDDLE (LIVE ITUNES VERSION).**

- ❖ Appreciate and value God's gifts.

- ❖ Don't dwell on other people's gifts; instead, appreciate and develop the ones you were born with.

- It's unwise and a slap in God's face to allow yourself to be distracted by other people's talent.

- **Practicing is better than preaching.**

- Practice then preach.

- Believe more in God than people.

- You are not lucky; you are blessed.

- **Although God has got you covered, he's still expecting you to be Godly even in trying situations.**

- There are tons of bitter people in your church and you might be one of them.

- Even though your heart might bleed because your children don't make the right spiritual decisions, you have to let them live their lives.

- **Trust yourself enough to believe in yourself.**

❖ Don't kid yourself, sin is stealing from your employer, being prideful, showing up to work late, cursing out your boss underneath your breath, cheating on your taxes, masturbation, telling little white lies, fornication, homosexuality, lust, swearing, narcissism, deceitfulness, robbing Peter to pay Paul, disrespecting your parents, drunkenness, envy, debauchery, laziness, selfishness, impatience, hostility, dissension, telling dirty jokes, jealously, procrastination, faithlessness, breaking promises to your children, anger, anxiety, ignorance, intolerance, and so on. With that said, which one of you has not sinned?

❖ **It's never too early or late to sit down and contemplate the spiritual decisions you have made in your life.**

❖ You *can't* and *shouldn't* blame others for where you are spiritually.

❖ The single, saved, and having sex mentality is dangerous.

❖ **Even though a situation might seem harmless, at any second it can**

explode into something harmful.

- Apart from God, you are weak and vulnerable in so many ways.

- **Just because you have the right to be a jerk doesn't mean you should exercise that right on a consistent basis.**

- Even in God, you will experience weaknesses, but you are powerful and strong enough to work through them.

- **Don't tell people the edited version of your life; instead, keep it one hundred.**

- Compassion is essential for understanding.

- **You should be evolving spiritually instead of revolving.**

SPIRITUALITY

- ❖ Upload the right material spiritually and download the wrong expeditiously.

- ❖ **If you believe and trust in God, it should be evident in your life.**

- ❖ Be careful which person you follow in the name of God.

- ❖ The Bible is your global positioning system (GPS) for getting to your destination.

- ❖ **Your character defines you.**

- ❖ The most audacious man you will ever meet in your life is God, and he can back up his audacity.

- ❖ **Don't focus on traditions; instead, focus on the right thing to do in spite of tra4ition.**

- ❖ Just because something is traditional doesn't mean it's still relevant in today's society.

- **Be careful what you feed your heart and mind.**

- It's difficult to regulate an evil heart.

- **If you think your heart is pure, you are lying to yourself.**

- Agape love is humanly possible.

- When your desires become your demands, you are in serious trouble.

- Some people choose not to want to know better.

- **MUSIC: "OH HAPPY DAY" BY THE EDWIN HAWKINS SINGERS**

- **Sometimes simply saying, "I am sorry," can do wonders to heal a broken friendship or relationship.**

- Sometimes a kind word can defuse a potentially explosive situation.

- **Consistently telling people they are going to hell isn't beneficial.**

- **VISIT: <u>WWW.BIBLOS.COM</u>**

- **Very few people will grasp the essence of life.**

MCKENZIE MCPHERSON

Did you get them all?

_ _ _   _ _   _ _

_ _ t _ _ _   _ _ _   _ _ _

_ _ _   _ _ _

_ _ _ _ _ r _ _ _ _ _

bitterne19s   **commul4ity**

g1515d   ran4om   l9ttle   addic20ive

se3urity   presid5ntial   ups20airs

sh21t up   ~~inte18action~~   **wol3en**

enviro14ment   adapt1ble   s5x   d1ys

b5fore   fr9days   emplo25ees

spou19e   fi7ht   **dem1nding**

mo19t   anyt8ing   child18en   m1nipulate

~~hur20ful~~   **withel8s**   beaut9ful

bl5ssed   bec1use   peo16le   sadne19s

beh9nd   tra4ition

LESSONS FROM GENERATION X TO GENERATION NEXT

Fun Facts about Author

Birthplace: Jamaica, West Indies

Astrology sign: Libra

Siblings: 2 (I'm the youngest)

Graduated high school at: 16

College: Fashion Institute of Technology (FIT)

College degree: Advertising, Marketing, and Communications

Favorite childhood memory: Dancing in the rain

Favorite music artists: Bob Marley, Sam Cooke, Aretha Franklin, Barbra Streisand, Whitney Houston, Michael Jackson, and Bing Crosby.

Best music for rainy days: Michael Buble / Old school reggae music (Jimmy Cliff, Pluto Shervington, Tenor Saw, Eric Donaldson, J.C. Lodge, Lt. Stitchie, Third World, Buju Banton, Yellowman, Barrington Levy, Cocoa Tea, Half Pint, Shelly Thunder, Chaka Demus and Pliers, Tony Rebel, Junior Reid, Shabba Ranks, Maxi Priest and Peter Tosh).

Favorite movies: Gone with the Wind, My Fair Lady, Witness for the Prosecution, The King & I, Carmen Jones, The Sound of Music, High Society, Love & Basketball, The Cardinal, Goodbye, Mr. Chips, An Affair to Remember, Houseboat, To Catch a Thief, Strangers on a Train, Guess Who's Coming to Dinner, Bullit, The Year of Living Dangerously, Dial M for Murder, and Inherit the Wind.

Favorite tv series: The Thorn Birds, The Cosby Show, The Jeffersons, Desmonds, Matlock, Perry Mason, A Different

World, Remington Steele, Moonlighting, The Golden Girls, and Law & Order.

Favorite websites: Time.com, Wikipedia.org, Youtube, and Huffington Post.

Twitter handle: @l_iv_e

Favorite place: Any place where I can find peace and silence.

Favorite sport: Track & Field

Favorite athlete: Muhammad Ali

Favorite colors: Red, magenta, canary yellow, or any color that is vibrant.

Guilty Pleasure: Being a *naughty* girl

Relationship status: It's complicated ☹

What I value most in a man: Character

Favorite gift from a man: A good hug (but I don't like hug and hold).

3 reasons I wear black: I'm feeling fat, going to a funeral, or going to confront someone who is messing with my money or state of mind.

Feel good song: "Man, I Feel Like a Woman" by Shania Twain

Can't Sleep: Listen to "Count Your Blessings" by Jimmy Durante

Short-term goal: To lose 85-100 pounds ☹ ☺

Long-term goal: To be the best I can possibly be.

I live for: My one moment in time ☺ ☺ ☺

Greatest fear: To die without fulfilling my God assigned purpose.

Greatest Pleasure: To finally accept me for me, flaws and all.

Favorite books of the Bible: Job, Proverbs, Ecclesiastes, and Romans.

Dream job: To be a chief invisible officer (CIO).

Want to make enough money: To take speech classes

Women I grew up admiring: Margaret Thatcher, Princess Diana, and Oprah Winfrey.

What I know for sure: There is a God, life is what you make it, no one ever wins in a war, and I can do bad all by myself.

What I want to be remembered for: Encouraging the awareness that one person can either revolutionize the world for better or worse but there is **ALWAYS** a choice.

That's All Love!!!

www.ingramcontent.com/pod-product-compliance
Lightning Source LLC
Chambersburg PA
CBHW032037090426
42744CB00004B/43